THE SINGLE MOM'S WORKPLACE SURVIVAL GUIDE

The Single Mom's Workplace Survival Guide

Brenda Armstrong

SERVANT PUBLICATIONS
ANN ARBOR, MICHIGAN

Vine Books in an imprint of Servant Publications especially designed to serve evangelical Christians.

Servant Publications—Mission Statement
We are dedicated to publishing books that spread the gospel of Jesus Christ, help Christians to live in accordance with that gospel, promote renewal in the church, and bear witness to Christian unity.

The stories in this book are true and have been used by permission.

Servant Publications
P.O. Box 8617
Ann Arbor, MI 48107
www.servantpub.com

Cover design: Paul Higdon, Minneapolis, Minn.

02 03 04 05 10 9 8 7 6 5 4 3 2 1

Printed in the United States of America
ISBN 1-56955-307-6

Library of Congress Cataloging-in-Publication Data

Armstrong, Brenda.
    The single mom's workplace survival guide / Brenda Armstrong.
        p. cm.
    Includes bibliographical references.
    ISBN 1-56955-307-6
    1. Single mothers–Life skills guides. 2. Single mothers–Employment.
3. Working mothers–Life skills guides. 4. Work and family. 5. Single mothers–
Religious life. I. Title.
    HQ759.915 .A76 2002
    646.7'8'0852–dc21

                                                                2002004336

Dedication

This book is dedicated to David and Alicia, my gifts from God and my reasons for surviving. You have taught me much more about life than I could ever teach you. You and grandson Christian are my rewards on earth. I love you.

—Mom

Contents

Foreword

Never in history has there been a greater number of single mothers raising children alone. Although the numbers have slightly decreased in recent years, single parents in America still head 26 percent of all families with children.[1] Of over twelve million single-parent households, single mothers head more than ten million.

Divorce and out-of-wedlock births contribute to the majority of these situations, but war, disaster, and the natural death of a spouse are other causes. On September 11, 2001, for example, through a despicable act of terrorism thousands of adults and children were suddenly thrust into the single-parent family lifestyle. As with most single-parent families, it was not by choice.

Clearly, most women do not enter marriage or become a parent with the idea that they are going to have to raise children alone. Because they no longer live in an age where parenting is a woman's primary occupation, many single mothers have worked outside the home or contributed to the household income. However, most find themselves unprepared to tackle the daunting tasks involved in being both the parent and the family provider.

Brenda Armstrong understands the single-parent struggle.

After ten years of a difficult marriage she became the sole provider for her two children—with only a high school education as preparation.

Now she sees and hears of the struggles of single parenting every day in her job as director of single-parent ministry for Crown Financial Ministries. I guarantee Brenda knows what it takes not just to survive but to flourish.

If you are a single mom who has found yourself struggling to survive, this book is for you. While single dads struggle with many of the same issues of raising children alone, their needs generally are different. Statistically they make more money than single mothers and have more support from family and friends. Their term of single parenthood is also generally shorter, because they tend to remarry more quickly than do single mothers.

Most single moms are in the parenting-alone stage for some time and, therefore, need to be prepared for the long haul. They need a survival guide.

The tools Brenda shares in this book will make a difference in your life. Yet the most important thing she will share with you is the hope that she and other single moms in your situation have found.

Larry Burkett
Gainesville, Georgia
January 2002

I would like to thank Karen Kubacki for being my ever-faithful assistant. She carried the load, as usual, while I worked on this book. I also appreciate Laura Petherbridge for providing her experience and input on the manuscript.

I would like to sincerely acknowledge the management of Crown Financial Ministries. A big thank you to Larry, Howard, and Dave for encouraging me to write the book. I am so grateful they recognize the importance of single parents and have a heart to help them.

To all the moms that wrote to tell me about their single-parent experiences: thanks for sharing your hearts. You made this book.

Thanks to my daughter Alicia and grandson Christian, who live with me. I know that we sacrificed family time while I wrote. I couldn't have completed it without their encouragement and support.

I would particularly like to thank Anita Palmer of Sam Hill Editorial Services for adding her much-needed insight. Her prodding kept this project on the right course and resulted in a much better manuscript.

Introduction

Like most little girls, I didn't grow up dreaming about becoming a single parent. I grew up wanting to get married and have children. I had creative aspirations, but they were secondary to my desire to become a wife and mother. My idea of marriage was a romantic fantasy.

My early childhood exposure to other families was 1950s television. However, my family reality was far from what I envisioned. My parents stayed together until death, but there was plenty of dysfunction in our home. My dad was an alcoholic. When I was seven he spent almost the entire year in detox. My mom was diabetic and was often hospitalized. The same year Dad was in detox she was institutionalized for tuberculosis. My sister, two brothers, and I spent that year in two different orphanages. The remainder of my first twelve years was spent in low-income housing projects—the first one was demolished because it had deteriorated so badly.

I was a bold child, not easily intimidated. Although our home was unpredictable and sometimes frightening, I always made sure that everyone knew what I wanted and heard what I was thinking. I was competitive and was often described as stubborn. These were not the most positive traits for little girls in the 1950s and early 1960s. Because of my intense feelings, I had a love-hate relationship with my dad. He was a lot of fun at times and terrifying at others. I became accustomed to the excitement and drama of the unpredictable lifestyle.

Both my parents were professed Christian believers. I knew that Mom loved God and had a real relationship with Jesus Christ. I was never sure about Dad. My folks sent their four children to church each Sunday on a bus. My older siblings were involved in church activities, but for some reason, I didn't have any involvement with other church families. One reason may have been the distance we lived from church. None of the neighbor families in the projects were good role models for my image of marriage.

My mom also may have contributed to my marriage fantasy. She would read classic fairy tales and poetry to me. I guess that's where the fantasy began. I really had no idea what a healthy family looked like, so I made it up. Of course, it involved a handsome man who would rescue me from my confusing family. We would have a nice home, two kids (a boy and a girl), a dog, and lots of romance. This kind of dream doesn't prepare you for marriage, let alone single parenthood.

My Broken Dream

I was on my own by the time I was eighteen because both Mom and Dad had died. My siblings were all married and starting their own families. I had no support from or involvement with the church. I was madly in love with a boy I had dated off and on through high school who did not want to commit to marriage. Grieving the loss of my parents and believing that any hope of that ideal family was slipping away, I found myself pregnant and alone at nineteen. In fear of losing my dream entirely, I married the first guy who asked.

The Family Pattern

At first, I didn't realize that I had chosen someone very much like my father. The family members of drug- or alcohol-dependent people tend to overcompensate and compromise themselves in order to prevent the addicted person from abusing. Since I grew up in an alcoholic home, my own dysfunction and full-blown codependency were enough to destroy any marriage, but I married a person with his own inappropriate passions, dependency, and dysfunction. It was a marriage without God, a relationship that was doomed to failure.

Being stubborn by nature, I hung in there. We had a second child and at times I believed we were happy. Yet I had to adapt my thinking so much to accommodate not upsetting my husband—and thus "causing" him to drink—that after ten years of marriage, my strong-willed personality literally had disappeared. I was facing the end of my marriage. My dream was shattered. I cried out to God, but I had long abandoned the relationship with him that started in my youth. I felt as though I was crying out to the ceiling and the ceiling was ignoring me. God must be very far away—did he even care? I had always been described as daring. Certainly I was a survivor by nature, willing to accept any challenge. Yet at that time in my life, I felt totally ill-equipped and lost. I didn't want my codependency patterns passed on to my children. I knew that I needed help if my children were to have any chance at a more normal life.

A Turning Point

God did answer my prayers, but not by changing my husband. My husband didn't want to change. I went through three years of professional counseling to break my codependency patterns. Part of my therapy required that I attend a support group. Through that group I met some Christians who seemed to have real relationships with God. They spoke to him as though he were right there in the room, and they really expected him to answer. They often talked about how he had answered their prayers. Although I grew up in a church, this was something I had never witnessed.

I had accepted the salvation message as a child, but God had always seemed far from me. Their God was there for them. He comforted them in their losses and helped them with their decisions. They discussed everything with him. I wanted what they had, and in a short time I discovered a relationship with Christ that I did not know was possible. In fact, the only hope I had at that time was in that new relationship.

As I started changing my patterns of behavior and focusing more on Christ, my husband decided he wanted no part of it and filed for divorce. I had only begun attending counseling and a support group when the marriage ended. I found myself with no self-esteem and plenty of fear, guilt, shame, anger, and bitterness. I had only a high school education and limited job skills. Talk about ill-equipped for survival! I had to start at the bottom.

No Survival Manual

For many years my work was primarily entry-level jobs. My kids endured being "latch-key" kids. My children say I was a good parent, but we had our struggles. I made mistakes. I didn't have a manual, and I had no single-parent role models. My friends were either single without children or married with children younger than mine, so they didn't know much more than I did about raising kids. In addition, the couples were without the baggage of divorce or codependency. Although they cared and helped when they could, they couldn't really understand my struggle to balance everything in my life.

Voices of Hope and Help

God intimately cared for my family through some very difficult times. There were many learning experiences. Through each lesson I learned more about his love and grew to trust him more. Following his guidance led me to a career, a healthy family, and contentment in other areas of my life. I know that he did not teach me for my benefit alone. He taught me so that I could share his lessons with those who would follow me.

We make lots of mistakes as single moms, but we do a lot of things right. I want you to benefit from what I and other single moms have learned so that you can minimize your errors. I have included the practical tools that have been the most helpful to me and others.

In this book you will have the opportunity to examine some of the reasons why you may be barely surviving. You will discover why you need to develop a healthy network of supportive relationships. You'll see ways to help bring balance between work and other areas of your life. And, finally, you'll find some practical tools to help you discover God's direction for work, survive at work, and manage the financial rewards of work.

My hope is that through prayer you will take these tools one by one and explore what kind of difference each one will make in your life. Seek godly counsel about any major decisions. Establish the recommended relationships. Take small steps toward making the changes. You will be on the way toward being a successful working single mom.

One
The Challenge: Understanding the Obstacles

Ilene is a single mother of four young children. This sweet young woman found herself alone after discovering her husband's drug abuse. She pleaded with him to get help; instead he left. Still separated after three years, Ilene sees little in monetary support and the children see even less of their father. Ilene doesn't have any unrealistic expectations that her husband will return, but she also doesn't believe that she should be the one to file for divorce.

Being a full-time mother before the separation did not prepare Ilene for the overwhelming job of working while caring for her family. Her education does not go beyond high school and she had worked very little outside the home. This mother believes that her highest priority is to be the best parent she can be, so upon examining her options, Ilene has decided to work at home taking care of other people's children. Hers is a modest income, to say the least.

Decisions like this are hard to make. Many moms suffer because it is so difficult to balance income, work, and children. For some mothers the decision to stay home may seem impossible. However, Ilene had the support she needed to make the decision. When Ilene lost her home, a close friend in another state allowed Ilene and her four children to live for a while with her family of six. This dear friend still helps Ilene with the children, when needed.

The friend introduced Ilene to a church that embraced her. One member of the church gave Ilene a car. Still another anonymously paid her rent for one year. Another put her in touch with a dentist who provided Ilene with much-needed and extensive dental surgery and implants at no cost to her.

Ilene was blessed to have such support. Yet like other single moms, she still must juggle a home, time with children, various activities, and work.

A Tough Job

Balancing family and a career while keeping your sanity is a challenge for any woman, not just single moms. Some mothers, both married and single, are still attempting to have it all while erroneously believing that no one in the family will suffer. Yet even in the best of two-parent families, having a career while being a mother is a balancing act. Sharing responsibilities with a supportive husband helps considerably, but still there are only so many hours in a day. In the end, somebody or something suffers. It may be the marriage, it may be the mother, or it may be the children.

Most healthy two-parent families realize this and try to share the responsibilities. Such families have a hard time when a spouse is out of town for a week or two—they can't imagine how tough it is to spend years raising children alone.

These brief separations can teach couples compassion for single parents. In fact, I know several single-parent ministries that were started by women who had temporary absences from their own spouse and were awakened to the difficulties of single parents.

Not in the Plan

The reason that parenting alone is so hard is because we weren't designed for it. God's plan for the family includes a father and a mother, and for a purpose: Two heads are better than one. The male and female perspectives differ and bring balance to the family. Children statistically do better emotionally, socially, and academically when both parents are in the home. God uses the design for the family as an example of how he loves us. He calls himself the Bridegroom of the church and asks individual believers to relate to him as a father. As a husband and father, he loves us, protects us, and provides for us as the husband would for the family. Even in this analogy, there is a mother or bride. It is the church. This bride is to fulfill the role of being the helpmate to God by loving and caring for his children.

God's design for the family doesn't guarantee success, but statistics bear witness that families with two biological parents in the home have a better chance for it. Because God designed the family with two distinct parental roles, a single mother or single father does not come already equipped for the job.

The good news is that God has made provision for the lack. We'll be looking at some ways in the next chapters. But first, it might help you to know you're not alone.

Your Company of Survivors

Today, many more parents are raising children alone. Single parents head one in four families with children in the United States. Most of those are single-mother households. Five years ago most mothers came into single parenting through divorce. Today, however, most single moms (42 percent) become single parents by having a child without being married.[1]

Since the 1970s, there has been more widespread societal acceptance of the never-married parent. In fact, today some celebrity and higher-income single women are applauded when they pursue single parenting by choice. Some of these affluent moms can afford to pay for live-in nannies to care for their children so they can continue their careers. Most single moms don't have that luxury.

Some single women choose to parent for worthy reasons like saving a child from foster care or a desperate living condition in a third-world country. Some choose single parenting because their biological clocks are ticking and they don't have a husband. Yet most never-married mothers become single mothers by accident and not by choice. They usually are in desperate situations and have been abandoned by boyfriends after making the decision to deliver and raise their children.

An Unwanted Situation

The divorced still make up a large part (40 percent) of the single mother population.[2] Many Christians assume that these "broken" marriages are a result of a fallen society and that this problem rarely affects people in the church. Sadly, however, that is not true. Christians divorce at the same rate as non-

Christians.[3] Nearly one out of every two marriages initiated this year will end in divorce, whether the couple is Christian or not.

Wives, not husbands, initiate most divorces.[4] Many of these women may have had good cause to separate. They or their children may have suffered unbearable circumstances of verbal, physical, sexual, or emotional abuse. Some women divorce due to what most Christians consider to be grounds for a "biblical divorce." They may have had a wayward husband who took off with another woman and refused to come home to his family. Or the husband may have left because he rejects God and the faith of his wife.

Some women divorce because they are selfish and want freedom from family responsibilities. But most divorced mothers do not want to be divorced. They are simply left to have the full responsibility for their families and have filed for divorce because the husband is no longer around.

A small percentage of women (5 percent) enter single parenting through the loss of a spouse. Obviously, these mothers planned on parenting with a partner.

No matter how you became a single parent, you most likely did not plan on raising your children alone. But now you are called upon to single-handedly juggle responsibilities that were meant for two people.

The Very Real Struggle

As mentioned, I have spent most of my life in single-parent homes, either heading one or living in one. My mother became a widow when I was fifteen years old, and I became a single parent after the divorce in 1982. I raised my children in a single-mother household from the time they were eight and ten years old. Currently, my single-parent daughter and grandson live with me.

Like some of you, my family endured some level of financial difficulties. Poverty is an issue for many single-parent families. In 1995, nearly six of ten children living in households headed by single women were near the poverty line.[5]

Like some of you, I have endured little support or involvement from the father of my children. Half the children in single-mother homes in America (forty million children) do not have regular involvement with their fathers, and half of those children have never even been in their father's home.[6] These are virtually fatherless children.

The impact of fatherlessness on children is dramatic. Children in single-mother homes are more likely to struggle academically, socially, and emotionally than children in two-parent families. They are more likely to use illegal substances or abuse drugs or alcohol. They tend to drop out of school more often. They tend to participate in socially alienated peer groups, delinquency, and criminal behavior. Daughters from single-mother homes have a greater tendency toward premature sexual activity and out-of-wedlock births. Seventy percent of young men in prison grew up without fathers.[7] These are horrible statistics, but they are not set-in-stone outcomes for your family.

Single Moms From Across the Country
In 2001 I heard from more than 150 single mothers across the United States who responded to a survey I had published in *Money Matters*, Crown Financial Ministries' monthly newsletter.

Although each family situation was unique, these moms faced many of the same issues and challenges that you and I face. Some had great support from their families or churches. Yet my heart broke for some of them, especially for those who had no support. Some of these women have struggled financially and emotionally. Some felt abandoned by everyone, including God, and believed that no one cared. Many expressed great apprehension about the fact that they alone were responsible for the outcome of their families.

Yet it doesn't have to be that way. For instance, Polly, a single mother in Baton Rouge, Louisiana, felt overwhelmed with the prospect of raising her son alone. She had no other choice but to work outside the home. For her, the greatest challenge was

---

...knowing that I was responsible for a roof over my child's head, clothing, food, day care, insurance, doctor visits. Because if I didn't, my son wouldn't have a home or food to eat. (Polly; Baton Rouge, Louisiana)

This single mom now has an eighteen-year-old son whom she has raised on her own since he was three. Polly discovered tools that helped her in her journey. She found a way to successfully balance work and family. According to this proud mom, the results were evident in her son, who "became valedictorian of his class, plays drums in a church band, and is awesome."

Like this mother, you likely didn't plan on this survival journey of balancing work and family. Single parenting was probably not your lifelong ambition. Like most single parents, you probably feel ill-equipped for the job. I know I did.

Plate Spinning

My longtime friend and associate, Barbara Schiller, author of *Just Me and the Kids*,[8] likens the single mom's balancing act to that of vaudeville plate spinners. These performers placed plates on the tops of poles of various heights, cheered on by the audience. The challenge was to keep all the plates spinning at once. The crisis came when more than one plate slowed down at the same time.

A single parent's life is trying to keep all the plates spinning at once. It helps to have a cheering audience who will assist you in keeping them going. You can do it, but it takes practice. You have to realize that there will be some broken plates, but that doesn't mean you're not a success.

Name Your Plate

Your spinning plates are probably very similar to those of other single moms. According to my informal survey, personal experience, and previous research, most of you are concerned about finding balance in relationships, time management, parenting, career, and finances. Balancing these areas of your life may leave you overwhelmed. You may be struggling with a lack of faith, lack of emotional support, guilt, fatigue, and loneliness.

To survive, you must have the tools you need. You can't spin a plate in midair. You need the pole. You can't spin a plate if you have only the pole. Your job and finances must be in balance or your work plates will fall. In this difficult game of survival you must recognize the areas you need to balance and the obstacles inherent in balancing them.

One of the keys to survival preparation is anticipating obstacles. You can't prepare for everything, but you can learn from others what to expect and how to avoid their mistakes. In my survey I asked women to share their biggest mistakes in single parenting. Respondents listed these:

- trying to keep up the former lifestyle
- guilt
- overcompensation with children
- debt
- depending on a man to save you
- not spending time with God
- not asking others for help

Any good survivalist will tell you that you need to anticipate hazards. Expect the unexpected. Like the Boy Scouts, we need to always be prepared.

The Raft Trip

This past summer three teenage boys, two of them sons of my co-workers, decided to make a short raft trip from one end of Lake Lanier in northern Georgia to the other. This U.S. Army Corps of Engineers' man-made lake is fairly large, with more than five hundred miles of irregular shoreline. The lake can be a dangerous place. There were many old structures and fences left on the valley floor when the lake was filled. A friend's husband disappeared and is believed to have drowned several years ago while managing a barge on the lake.

The raft trip was planned to take three days. The normal hindrances for navigation on the lake are weather and other marine craft. Yet this year, the water level was eight feet below normal due to two years of drought in the region, which presented more hazards in the water.

However, these brave, soon-to-be high school seniors were Eagle Scouts. Having grown up in scouting, they had plenty of training in survival. Before they launched their raft, they spent considerable time developing their plan. In fact, the raft was the third they had made.

My co-worker, a seasoned Scout leader, helped his son and friends design and build the watercrafts, including the deluxe final version, which was complete with subdeck compartments, ten fifty-five-gallon drums for flotation, and a sixteen-foot mast and matching sail. The local paper and radio covered the boys' Huck Finn adventure. As the raft pulled from shore that Friday morning, thunder rolled and rain began.

On Sunday the boys returned, exuberant and safe. How were they able to be successful? Because they were equipped. They were experienced outdoorsmen. They had researched what worked for others. They had tested and they had a plan. As true Boy Scouts, these boys were prepared.

If you are going to survive this single-parent jungle, you will need to be prepared. Taking time to discover your challenges will greatly influence your ability to overcome them. I know it is tough.

I don't know where you and your children are, but I can assure you, your family doesn't have to contribute to another negative single-parent family statistic. Whether or not you have support, your family can survive, and thrive. The testimonies and tips provided in this book provide the tools. The rest is up to you.

Two
The Buddy System: Why Two Are Better Than One

One of the greatest keys to survival is having the right support system. Think about it. You are doing a job that was meant for two people. Do you expect to be able to handle it all by yourself? Yet you don't swim alone; you don't camp alone. There are numerous activities that you wouldn't do alone. Why? Because you need to have a buddy there to help you in case of an emergency. As a single mom, you no longer have a built-in buddy. If you're drowning and no one is alongside, you're lost.

Being alone is one of the biggest obstacles to your survival. You may be drowning and not even know it. Sure, you may be prepared to tackle some issues alone, but along the way, you will find times when you have a great need for others. I'm going to give your survival rate a big boost right now, with the most-mentioned tip from successful single mom survivors: Don't take this journey alone.

Successful single moms know that you have to develop a support system to survive.

The Obstacles

There are single moms who know they shouldn't be doing this alone, but don't know what else to do. Then there are some who go it alone because they want to try to solve their problems themselves. Yet they are doing so in the face of tremendous hindrances that they may not even recognize. These obstacles cloud perspective and contribute to wrong or even disastrous choices.

Depending on a Man to Save You

In my experience, moms tend to be out of balance on the issue of having men in their lives. Some women lean toward a radical feminist viewpoint and reject the value of marriage entirely. They can make it alone and they don't need anyone interfering. However, these women may not be as strong as they appear. Often independent women are masking deep wounds and keep their distance from men to protect themselves from further hurt.

Most of the single moms with whom I have contact lean the other way, however. They are too dependent. This kind of mom thinks that she can't survive without a man in her life.

Neither of the above views is correct. Going it alone is hard. It is easy to assume that if you had just one more set of hands and another income you could make it. You may long for the physical relationship you experienced with your children's father. If only you could find Mr. Right.

So many single moms I know (yes, even Christian ones) are so focused on finding "Mr. Right" that they aren't giving their all to the Lord and to their children. I've been guilty of this on occasion, but thankfully the Lord (along with my accountability partner) has kept me in line and put me back on the "straight and narrow." (Tamy; Chambersburg, Pennsylvania)

Friends, family members, and even some church members might contribute to this angst by encouraging parents to match up. They unwittingly assume that an absent husband can be replaced and that this replacement will take care of the family (and then they won't have to). Yet remarriage is not the easy answer that it appears to be. In many cases it can destroy your family.

Although God has put some healthy blended families together, this is the exception rather than the norm. Statistics show that most remarriages end in divorce, especially when children are involved.[1] Children do not accept stepparents easily; and parents tend to favor biological children over stepchildren, and sometimes, over a spouse. There also are higher instances of abuse in stepfamilies.

If you are dating or considering dating, think carefully about the implications of exposing your children to someone to whom they may become attached. Many children in single-parent homes have been through a lot of heartache and loss and don't need to lose another important relationship. If you are dating primarily for companionship without intent to marry, it is best if you don't involve the children. Yet my question is, why are you dating if you are not looking for marriage? You can get yourself into some difficult situations when you date.

If you are dating with marriage in mind, you need to consider when would be the appropriate time to involve the children. A courtship involving parents with children should be a long courtship. Young children adapt more readily to a blended family than teenagers do, because teenagers are less likely to accept a new "parent" in the home.

Some women don't bother with marriage. Instead, they compromise their morals by cohabiting with a boyfriend. Granted, the primary reason women do this is because they fear the great financial and parenting challenges of raising children alone.

Avoid compromising your beliefs by "living with" a boyfriend to survive economically. I did this as I felt I had no other options that made sense. But I paid a price emotionally and spiritually. When I left him and made a "fresh start" on my own (with nothing but bags and boxes to put my meager belongings in and a temporary place to live for me and my two sons) ... God richly blessed me and he is my provider! (Bonnie; Toms River, New Jersey)

If you do not observe celibacy, it will ruin your chances of finding another life partner—and you cannot serve as a good example for your kids. All my non-Christian friends encouraged me to go out and "have a love life" once I was single. It goes without saying that it's very important to pick your friends carefully. (Lisa; Parkville, Maryland)

Yes, God does intend for families to include fathers. Yet he doesn't want you to compromise your values to provide one. God promises that he will be a father to the fatherless and a husband to the widow. Basically, he is promising that you will have what you need if you're raising children alone. Sometimes he provides directly through inspiration or strength; other times he uses people to become his hands and meet your needs. God is the only one who can rescue you. Women who trust a man to save them often end up adding to the overwhelming divorce rate of second and third marriages.

If God should bring a partner for you, you have a better chance of survival if you start your marriage with two emotionally healthy people. So, your first goal should not be finding a man. It should be to get healthy.

Falling Into the Guilt Trap

A sense of guilt or failure is a common trait among single moms—failure at marriage or relationships, failure at parenting, failure at financially providing for the family. Guilt is a trap. It keeps you from fully living in the present.

The greatest challenge for me was trying to overcome the great guilt I felt for not being there for my children—having to tell them no, I couldn't go to their field trips because I had to work, and having to leave my baby all day with a stranger while I was somewhere I didn't want to be! (Tera; Mascoutah, Illinois)

Don't get caught in the guilt trap of being both parent and superwoman. Your kids aren't going to remember that your house looked like Better Homes and Gardens; *they will remember the time you invested in their activities. (Debbie; Delta, Colorado)*

You need to realize that you cannot be it all or do it all. You can't be all things to all people. You are not superwoman (who, by the way, never really existed). Guilt is a feeling that is very difficult to overcome alone. If you are struggling with guilt, you may need to share your feelings with others that have overcome this challenge or with a professional counselor.

When we feel guilty, we feel shame and tend to isolate ourselves from others. We believe that by avoiding other people we can avoid the shame. Although we don't like isolation, it is a kind of protection. It keeps us from dealing with the input of others. Thus we carry all the responsibility alone. This is not God's plan.

Bitterness

So many women are functioning under bitterness. Because they didn't ask for their situations, it is hard to let go of the feeling of being a victim. I'm not saying that you may not have truly been wronged. I am saying that holding bitterness against a person, a situation, or God can destroy you and your family. Forgiveness does more for you than it does the other party.

The Answer

We've said that God designed the family to include a mother and a father to effectively support the family and raise the children. The obvious question, then, is how does one person do what was meant for two people? If you are not equipped for the job, how is it possible? Single moms may feel as though they are abandoned to deal with all of the responsibility, but this is only true to an extent.

Like the vaudeville plate spinners, if you want to keep all of your plates spinning at once, you need to have accountability in your life to help direct your attention to the falling plates. That means you need a buddy. You need someone you can trust with your pain.

There is only one partner I know of who can guarantee your survival. Without this companion, there is little hope. Many successful single parents have learned the secret of this relationship. Others struggle in disappointment because they depended on people who have let them down.

Primary Companion

There is only one source, one main supporter, and one primary companion. The only partner who will never leave or forsake you is God. When all else fails, God doesn't. When people fail, God doesn't. We can trust him. He constantly supplies what we need. God must be your primary companion on this journey.

This may be a new concept for you. You may never have heard about God's love and care for you and your family. God has a special place in his heart for the single-parent family.

Are you familiar with James 1:27? "Pure and undefiled religion in the sight of our God and Father is this: to visit orphans and widows in their distress"(NASB). Your situation is not a surprise to him. The literal meaning of *widow* in this passage indicates the idea of deficiency, a woman lacking a husband, literally or figuratively.[2] God knew the time would come when there would be many women raising children alone, and he commanded his people to care for them.

If fact, this duty was so important in Old Testament times that there were consequences to not caring for these women and children. Deuteronomy 27:19 says, "Cursed is he who distorts the justice due an alien, orphan, and widow" (NASB).

Single-mother families have a special place in God's heart. And that same God of the Bible wants to be your primary companion. He made provision for you before you were even born and before you became a single mom.[3] If you have not done so before, pick up a Bible and begin reading in John, the fourth book of the New Testament. You will discover a great love, greater than any you can have with a man.

He Will Be Husband and Father

God is willing to fill the role of both husband and father in your family. It may seem incomprehensible when you can't see him or hear him. I learned this concept when I was unable to provide some things my son needed. At one point he only had worn-out jeans to wear to school, and they were not worn out in the popular places. He skipped school for several days before I was notified. When I asked why he wasn't attending school, he answered that he was ashamed to go because the other kids made fun of his clothes. I couldn't do anything about buying him new clothes at the moment, so I told him to ask his father—his heavenly Father. The very next week a woman at work offered us three bags of nearly new boys' pants. She had three sons who had outgrown them and wanted someone to get some wear out of them. These were designer clothes—much better than I would have bought if I had had money.

God often supplied what my children needed without any help from me. As I entrusted their material needs to God, they eventually learned to trust him for all their needs. He truly cares about you and your children. Allow him to fill that empty place.

Give your life to God. He can be a father, husband, all you need for your family. (April; Bedford, Indiana)

Remind yourself that God is a father to the fatherless and that he promises in Isaiah 54 that he is your husband. I have volumes to tell about having him as my husband, especially in the area of finances. Watch daily for God's blessings in your life and the lives of your children. Remember that God's favor is real and it does go before you into every situation. (Gail; Virginia Beach, Virginia)

Communication With Your Primary Partner

Communicating with God is not hard. Prayer is communication with God, but prayer is not always piously bowing down and folding your hands, although those focused times are very important. Prayer can also be conversations when you share every thought and concern with God in bits and pieces throughout the day.

> Because it is our communication with God, prayer keeps us in touch with the source of everything we need. Prayer gives us hope, confidence, assurance, and a chance to reaffirm our reliance on God. Through prayer, we seek the wisdom and the strength to make right choices and to find God's will in difficult situations. Prayer relieves us of burdens by enabling us to lay them before God. Prayer gives us a channel for praise and thanksgiving when we pass milestones or travel through a stretch of beautiful country. Without prayer, our entire journey is in jeopardy.[4]

True communication means being real with God. You can tell him anything. I remember one single mom who called me about her struggles. She told me about a very disturbing financial situation she was facing, and her strong feelings about how unfair it was. I asked her if she had talked to God about it. She was shocked. "I could never tell God this! It is too ugly!" she said.

I guess she thought that he would think less of her or that he couldn't handle her feelings. She seemed to feel guilty about feeling that the situation was unfair. I told her that God already knew how she felt. She might not have had answers to her prayers because she hadn't asked God to answer them. I told her to tell him honestly how she felt about the situation, to yell if she had to. Or cry. Or scream. But to be honest. Then to ask for wisdom. This was an unheard-of concept for her.

A few days later the mom called back. She said she had taken my advice. She went to the garden where no one could hear her and started telling God how she felt. She described her prayer as soft and polite at first, but remembering that God already knew, her prayers changed.

> Boy, did I let him have it! Wow! I can't describe all the emotion and pain that came out. But you were right. God could handle it. I guess he did already know.

And the result? Though it doesn't always happen this way, she said that an answer to her prayer came as soon as she returned to the house. Now the situation is settled, at least from her perspective.

Give everything to God and he will take care of everything. (Jean; city unknown)

Pray hard about everything. Ask for clarity. (Terrie; Simi Valley, California)

You can be real with God when you talk to him. Prayer can be solemn at times. But at other times you will need to let God know how you really feel. God can't take your pain if you don't give it to him. He already knows it's there; he's just waiting for you to let it go.

This vital relationship with God takes effort. If God is truly your primary companion, then you have to take the time and effort to share your concerns with him. But the difference it makes is worth the time involved. It makes all the difference in your survival.

No matter what you have to sacrifice (usually sleep)— spend time in God's Word and with our Lord every day. Many of my friends never miss a workout, but couldn't find their Bible if I asked them to. Pray for God's guidance and wisdom daily. He is faithful and he will grant this! (Tamy; Chambersburg, Pennsylvania)

Always keep your focus on the Lord. I can tell when I start to get too busy and things start to unravel because my time spent with him has become less frequent. (Debbie; Delta, Colorado)

You can count on God to answer. You may not ever hear an audible voice—few people have. Yet you can often sense a prompting after praying, while praising him, or when reading the Bible. You will learn to discern when God is prompting you when you see whether the results were of God. Expect him to answer.

Go to God's Word first with the attitude of fully expecting God to give you direction. Be open to the Holy Spirit. (Lynda; Ontario, Canada)

Keeping a journal will help you see God's answers. It will help you remember his faithfulness when times are trying. You can return to it again and again. I often counsel single moms about finances. If they don't keep a journal, the first thing I ask them to do is to write down what God has done for them, even if it is in list form. This helps them to see how God has already cared for them and gives them faith that he will continue to do so.

> Keep a journal about how the Lord works in your life each day. (This is one I am working on.) Don't journal about all of the pains and struggles like I have done for so long, but rather about God's love and faithfulness! Make time to worship the Lord daily. (Denise; Bloomington, Indiana)

Your Burden Bearer

Larry Burkett always asks, do you trust God or do you just say that you trust God?

Many people say that they are Christians, that they know and trust God, but they really don't. Sometimes it is because they want to keep control over part of their lives. Another reason may be that they simply don't know what part God is supposed to handle and what part they are responsible to handle and they cross the line in handling God's part.

There are burdens that we should bear, and God has equipped us to handle them. He provides the strength and ability to do what we need to do. Then there are burdens that are too big for us to carry. Admitting our inability to do it all doesn't mean that we are weak. It provides God the opportunity to carry all the burdens that are too heavy for us to bear. That is a great relief—if we can believe it.

I often see and speak with many single moms that add heartache to their lives because they feel their life is over once they are alone.... We must take the time to carefully sort out what has happened in our lives, allow the Lord to sort out our emotional pain, and give him every avenue of emotion we can't handle. God blessed me with supportive family and church friends but many times, God is the only one we can turn to for guidance, for comfort, for strength, for direction. (Laura; El Centro, California)

To access the strength of the Lord to bear our burdens, we must constantly acknowledge our weakness, and then walk in confidence of what he has provided or strengthened us to do.

Sometimes we walk in our own confidence instead of the confidence that comes from acknowledging our weakness and we cross the line between our responsibility and God's. That is where the struggle begins—when we're trying to do something that we have not been equipped to do.

Have you ever observed a person who is tone-deaf but is trying to sing? It's pretty sad. There are always people who will encourage the individual not to give up and to keep trying, even when the lack of ability is evident. This is futile when God has not equipped the person with a clear ability to sing. I have a relative who went through a series of voice lessons to overcome this lack. Her joyful noise unto the Lord is now more pleasant for those around her, but she never became a skilled soloist. God provides the equipment we need to survive if we are doing what God wants us to do. He is the only one who can, and he does it only if it pleases him and his purposes for our lives.

In case you didn't know, God does have a purpose for your life. When you are able to grasp hold of this, you will have grasped one of the best survival tools.

Jeremiah 29:11 says, "'For I know the plans I have for you,' declares the Lord, 'plans to prosper you and not to harm you, plans to give you hope and a future.'"

This is God's assurance to his children. He has the ability and the resources to get you where you need to be, to equip you not only to survive, but to thrive.

Learning to Trust

You may believe, like some, that your life is too much of a mess for God to save. You may feel guilty or like a failure, but you are not beyond God's ability to save. If you earnestly seek him with a repentant heart, and acknowledge your part in anything you have done to cause or aggravate your situation, God will hear and answer. God's plan of salvation is clearly spelled out in his Word, the Holy Bible.

If you already believe in God's salvation and you are still struggling, it doesn't necessarily mean that you have done something wrong. It doesn't mean that God is punishing you or your children for your single-parent situation. There are consequences to sin and God does allow us to suffer those consequences. Like any loving parent, he wants us to learn from our mistakes and if possible, from the mistakes of others. Be assured, however: he does have the ability to deliver you. If he allows your situation, then he has a reason.

It is easy to see in hindsight why I struggled. God did have a plan to use my life to help others, but more than that, God wanted me to learn to trust him, and him alone. I went from being overconfident in my youth to having no confidence as an adult. As I began to grow in Christ, I began to regain confidence. Yet I fluctuated from "I can do everything myself" to "I just can't handle anything!"

The balance came when I learned that "I can do everything through Christ." Do you know what that means? Do you really understand that? It doesn't mean that you are now equipped to be super-mom and super-employee, or that you will be perfect and everyone will love you. It means that God will equip you to do what he calls you to do and he will provide the strength to do it. That is why his "burden is light and his yoke is easy." The alternative is that if you do it on your own you will be carrying more than God equipped you to carry and you won't succeed.

He Is Your Provider
Some of us didn't ask to be sole providers for our families—the role was thrust upon us. It bears repeating that God is the only one who can provide all that you need. The testimony of other single moms confirms it.

Please don't forget to pray for whatever the need is: direction, finances, health, loneliness. God wants to help you. (Betty; Camdenton, Missouri)

> *Pray. God always provides. And have faith that he will. (Linda; Ontario, Canada)*

The problem we often have in trusting God's provision and equipping is that we fail to recognize what he has already done and is doing in our lives. That old adage "count your blessings" is not trite. It is a tried and true practice of content believers. What are you thankful for today? If you have health, thank God. If you have a roof over your head today, thank God. If you have food today, thank God. If you have the joy of spending time with your children today, you have a wonderful blessing. If you are able to get up today, thank God. If you made mistakes yesterday, thank God you can start over again today. If God has helped or delivered you in any way, from harm, from illness, from anything, count it a blessing. You will see that once you begin, the list goes on and on.

Three
Where Are Your Buddies?
Finding the Support You Need

We've established that your support network starts with your primary partner, who is God. Yet you will also need to build a network of people who will provide input and support in your journey of survival. These are the people that God places in your life to help you. Some have more responsibility for supporting your family than others do. I call this the hierarchy of provision.

Levels of Support

First, each person has responsibility to provide for his or her own family, which includes your children and yourself. You must seek God for all of your family's needs. He provides you with the wisdom, skills, and ability to provide for your own household.

Second, God provides for your needs through your natural family. That includes your extended family members, brothers, sisters, parents, and other relatives.

When the extended family is not able or willing to help, then the church is the third level of support. The Bible says that the church is to provide for women who are "widows indeed." This term means women who are alone without the support of a husband or natural family. The "church" may mean a group of believers from one organized church or individual believers that God sends to help. When the local church body will not help, then God may send help through other means or people.

Many women start out disadvantaged because they find themselves ostracized from family or friends when they become single moms. They have already endured the heartbreak or rejection by being abandoned, either by the death of a husband, through rejection, or through a lack of commitment. Now they must endure rejection from family or friends who have the "you made your bed, now you lie in it" attitude. It is not easy to trust people when those you need and trusted most let you down. Losing trust causes us to develop either an "I can do it myself" attitude or a "nobody cares" attitude. We don't let people too close because we have been hurt.

I think we have lost our trust, being single. We just assume that we are on our own. If you're sick, call a friend to pick up cough drops! Don't take yourself out. You would do it for them, let them do it for you! (Kathy; Swansea, Illinois)

Your situation may be unique, but your needs are common among single moms. You need acceptance, but you don't need to be a victim. There is help available if you will step outside your isolation and look for it.

Reach out for help if you need it. (Amy; Lilburn, Georgia)

Don't try going at this alone. I tried and it does not work. Seek out help. If help is offered, take it. Use help from family and the church. (Nanette; Winder, Georgia)

This network of support looks different for each person.

Family

Some relationships endure anything. I hope you have at least one or two of those in your life. Hopefully, it is family members who will stand by you and love you no matter how many mistakes you've made. If your extended family is nearby and you have a good relationship with them, they can be a great source of help to you.

Parents and siblings often make good advisors and may be able to help with financial and practical needs. Many families are willing to swap child care or provide child care for little or no pay. Holidays with family are special, just because you have the people who care about you around to share those days with you. The time you spend with family almost always has a dual purpose. You help them and they help you. Plus, keeping these relationships helps the children feel connected. Some new single moms have found a move closer to family very beneficial.

After the divorce, I lost my home and had nowhere to go. I didn't have parents to turn to, and my brothers and sister did not live near me. So I moved back to my hometown. My sister and her husband opened their home to my children and me for a ten-month stay while I established myself in a job. We would have been homeless if it were not for family.

I have a wonderful network of family and friends that I can vent to. Sometimes, you just have to let out your frustration, verbally, and get it out of your system. But on the other hand, you have to drop it once you've vented. It doesn't do anyone any good to keep hashing and rehashing problems you cannot change. (Sheila; Downers Grove, Illinois)

My parents are wonderful. I would not have survived if it hadn't been for them. They never interfered with what I did or how, but were always available to talk to, make suggestions, and watch the kids. (Linda; Ontario, Canada)

My own single-parent daughter lives with me. I can provide a home for her and her son while she continues her education. We have struggled to relate to each other as adults instead of as parent and child, but after a few years, we developed a very close, supportive relationship.

Keep your children in close proximity to your parents and family if at all possible and spend time with them. I had great support from family. My parents helped with day care. One sister came to live with us and share expenses and fellowship. (Sharon; Round Rock, Texas)

Keeping strong relationships with family will benefit both you and your children. Yet even if family is far away or unwilling to be involved, there are other sources for building relationship support.

The Church
It is important to your survival for you to be in a supportive environment. My hope is that you find it in a local church. After family, the church is the entity that God has designed to meet your needs. A support system made up of people from church benefits both you and your children. It is very important to find a Bible-believing and teaching church so that you and your children will have the spiritual support that you need. Yet it is also important to find a church where you feel accepted and loved.

> *The church is a very big part of my children's lives. I get strength from attending Sunday school and church. I just don't know how other single parents can cope without having the Lord in their life. (Julie; Belleville, Illinois)*

> *One of the first things that I did after my divorce and relocating to a new city was to join a church. My church body became my main support system. (Jan; Glendale, Arizona)*

A good sign of a caring church is one that has an established benevolence ministry or practical helps ministry to meet the needs of people both inside and outside the church. Care should go beyond saying hello or "I'll pray for you, have a nice day." People should be personally involved in your family's life. You should feel like part of the church. When you or another member has a need, the church should be responsive and provide help whether or not a benevolence program is in place.

Churches can offer assistance with finances, or provide services in home repair, child care, or car maintenance. Clothing and food distribution is another practical way the church can help. Other adults can become mentors for you and your children.

Some churches may appear to be uncaring because the membership has never been taught how to help people with unique needs. If you know that there are people who want to help, but don't know how, educate your church by sharing what you need or by encouraging the leadership to get training[1] on how to help meet practical needs.

We were especially fortunate to feel like we were a part of our church family. Activities at our church were not mainly geared to two-parent units where we would have felt like misfits. Furthermore, the men in at least three of the churches we attended over the years actually became excellent mentors and role models for my sons. (God in his miraculous way allowed the loss of their earthly father and replaced him with himself and a handful of "other fathers.") (Patty; Collegeville, Pennsylvania)

The church that led me to Christ gave me a $200 love gift after I had been there only several weeks. The money meant more to me spiritually than the needed help it provided. That $200 kept me in church. How could I walk away from people who gave so easily to me? I had not asked for the money, only for prayer that God would provide. (Barbara; Bayfield, Colorado)

If your church is not supportive of single parents and doesn't include them in the church's activities, you need to see if they will work on their acceptance and support. If they will not, then start looking for another church home. There are caring churches out there. I know. I hear from them every day.

My church was very helpful to me for the first two years. They paid several mortgage payments for me; a group of men put a new roof on my house; another group painted the outside of it for me. After I found a job, a group of women volunteered to help me. One would call me every Saturday to see if I needed anything the next week. If I didn't, they would bring me a meal. (Linda; Asheville, North Carolina)

Sometimes, though, the problem doesn't lie with the church. Sometimes it lies with the single mom. Isolation is deadly. The feeling of being different sometimes keeps you from getting the support that you so desperately need. The closer you become with your support network, the better they will understand you and your needs.

I know that I tend to isolate myself because I feel I would be judged by women in "traditional" roles in the church and seen as some sort of "disadvantaged" person. It can be very challenging to find a place in a church full of married couples. (Chandra; Schwenksville, Pennsylvania)

Don't be afraid to use help that is offered to you. It doesn't mean you can't handle things yourself. It means you are smart enough to see that a little help can go a long way toward your sanity. (Dawn; Dothan, Alabama)

You know that you need people. Yet the people you need in your support system may need some sensitivity training from you before they can begin to understand what your needs are and how to effectively help you with them. This seems selfish, but it is not. Open communication builds awareness. What they learn from you will help them deal with other people in need.

Sensitize your family, friends, and church to all your needs, especially if you are the only [single mom] in your church. Reach out to other single moms and widows. They know similar pain and loneliness. (Karen; Sweet Valley, Pennsylvania)

Peer Groups
One way to get over the isolation barrier is to connect with other single moms. Finding others who understand and have "been there" is a great support for single parents. The problem is that many churches reach out to single parents through singles ministries, but these ministries are not going to meet the needs of most single moms.

Over the years, churches have become more welcoming to singles, especially those who are divorced. Many more of them are offering divorce recovery groups to invite single parents into the church. This has worked very well for many single adults. However, since most single moms have never been married, the church will need to adapt its divorce recovery ministry to accommodate all relationship recovery.

After a divorce or relationship recovery class, most attendees are ushered into the singles class or group. For single adults without children that may be fine, but that may not be the case for single moms. Any single parent can tell you, single adults are not the same as custodial single parents. Single parents are parenting alone. Single is an adjective; parents are what they are. It just doesn't make sense to me. Churches don't realize that they are putting the people with the most financial and family responsibility in with the people with the least financial and family responsibility.

Don't get me wrong. There are some great, spiritually sound singles groups. I am very supportive of them. But I am not sure that single mothers who are trying to balance raising children and work have the time or energy to keep up with the singles. The single adults in the group that I led ate out before church, after church, during events, and many times in between. The singles could afford rafting and skiing trips. Plus, there is always the vulnerability issue. Many single parents are unknowingly looking for that man to rescue them and the availability factor of people in a singles group leads to matching up, even if that is not the intent of the group leaders. Wounded women need to avoid this situation. Many vulnerable women have become involved with the wrong men in good Christian singles groups.

Finding a church with a single-parent group is difficult

because there still aren't that many out there. A church usually has to be fairly large before it invests staff in a single-parent ministry. Because there is no place for them to fit, 95 percent of the single-parent population does not attend church regularly.[2] So finding support from other single parents is a challenge.

Join a support group at church or in the community. The greatest resource a single parent can have is another single parent. (Linda; Decatur, Georgia)

Connect with other single moms and be vulnerable and willing to give of yourself. (Portlynn; Atlanta, Georgia)

Many single moms that are unable to find single parent support often find support in women's groups. Yet others feel rejection from married women because they believe that the married women fear the single parent is a threat to them or their marriages. Some of the women who responded to my survey (mentioned in chapter 1) were part of a church when they divorced. They said they lost married couple friends in the process. Since most single parents feel rejection from two-parent families, getting this support is very difficult. One way to overcome this perception is to befriend two-parent families, ideally with children the same ages as your children.

I don't believe that most healthy couples feel threatened by a single mom. I believe that they don't understand her loneliness or the need to be with other families. The perception of the church is partly responsible for this lack of understanding. Since they classify single parents as singles, they believe that all their needs can be met in a singles group. As we have discussed, that just isn't true.

On the other hand, many single moms have successfully befriended couples. Healthy couples do not make the single parent feel like a fifth wheel. They don't try to play matchmaker. Furthermore, they never allow husbands to spend time alone with the single mom. If the husband is to help the single mom with something in the home, the wife comes along. If a meal is to be shared, it should be in a family setting unless it is just for the ladies.

Fathers in two-parent families should be encouraged to include the kids of single parents when planning outings for their own children. Two-parent families can be good role models for you and your children. This involvement helps you and your children learn to trust again when you see men treating their wives and children in a loving and supportive manner.

Do not be afraid to mix with couples. You need the care and input. Also, your child needs to see healthy two-parent homes. (Hendy; Ontario, Canada)

Don't pull away from your married friends, assuming they will no longer love, relate, or want anything to do with you. My biggest fear was that my married friends would no longer be my friends. In fact, the opposite was true. They rallied around me and prayed, cried, and provided for me. I couldn't have survived without them. (Jennifer; Johnson City, New York)

My daughter befriended a two-parent family that decided to take my grandson along with them on their family vacation this past summer. This family has three children; the oldest was going into fourth grade, the same as my grandson. They spent a week at the beach, and my grandson, who has never met his father, spent Father's Day for the first time with a stand-in dad. Another man in our church has raised his own sons and is now mentoring younger boys. He takes my grandson and a teenage boy to breakfast now and then. He occasionally comes to my grandson's ballgames and makes sure my grandson is involved in church activities for men and boys.

Developing relationships with older couples or women with grown children provides another source for mentors with parenting experience to share, and potential caregivers who may be willing to keep a sick child for you.

Talk to wise older women and listen to what they have to say, particularly grandmothers and mothers who have raised godly children. They can tell you things from good healthy meals to prepare on a low budget to tips on how to shop wisely or getting your kids to share the workload around the house. (Patricia; Cleveland Heights, Ohio)

Church is a great place to economize your time for friendship and service. You can attend the adult classes while your children go to their age-appropriate classes. Choose your adult class wisely. Make sure it is a fit for you and your single-parent lifestyle, socially, emotionally, and financially. Consider waiting a while before joining a singles class. Maybe when the children are older and spending more time with youth or teen activities you will have more time and resources to participate in singles' activities. In the meantime, don't be afraid of developing relationships with couples with children the same ages as your children. You will have more in common. You can share parenting concerns and tips, swap child care, attend events together, or perhaps even share vacations.

Small Groups

Peer groups are wonderful for finding others in your situation, but small groups also are an open door to relationships with people who are different from you. If your church supports a small group ministry of any kind, get involved. Don't be afraid to open up to people with different circumstances.

You have the opportunity to both give and receive in a small group and to build lasting friendships.

At the time of my divorce, I was involved in a small group ministry at my church. They were a lifesaver to me. They listened to me, provided help and advice when asked, and prayed for me. If it hadn't been for my small group, I wouldn't be where I am today. My small group included me in all activities and helped me not to feel like an outcast. They also helped me with minor home repairs and advised about car problems. (Rosemary; Huntsville, Alabama)

I tried to rely upon my devices too many times before and failed. I knew that only God could make something good out of this mess. I remembered from the Crown [Financial Ministries adult small group] study that godly counsel could be a big help, so that is what I looked for. All I ever wanted was to do what God wanted me to do. God is still in the miracle business. Just ask me. (Cyndi; Haysville, Kansas)

As important as support is for single moms, that isn't their greatest concern; they desperately want role models for their children. Some desire a strong male influence for their children because the fathers are either absent, not involved, or are poor role models. Others want family mentoring so that their children will see how God designed the family and witness it working. This can be accomplished by fellowshipping in a diverse small group.

Close Friendships

Friends are a very important part of your survival. You need people you can trust who will accept you as you are. Friendships at work are good, but most moms don't have much time to pursue them after work. In addition, Christian single moms need to protect themselves from ungodly influences they may encounter with co-workers.

Christian friends provide a natural network. You help meet each other's needs. If your friend can't help you, he or she may know someone who can. Your friends should be encouraging to be around. If you feel consistently depressed or drained with a friend, you need to find a new friend. You don't have the time or emotional resources to carry someone else.

Seek a support system of one or two trusted friends, which may or may not be family members. Commit to sharing, with only this support team, your innermost thoughts and concerns. Without a marriage partner to talk things over with, we do have the need to hash over problems, plans, fears, and dreams with someone. Avoid sharing these things with too many people. If that is all you can talk about to other people, you are going beyond the need to verbalize your thoughts into a "woe is me" life. (Mary Ann; Penn Yan, New York)

Roadblocks to Healthy Relationships

Overcompensation

When you perceive you or your children as suffering, the tendency is to overcompensate for the loss. Your own pain and guilt will lead you to try to make up for all the lack.

Many moms try to make up for their inability to be there and to do it all by overspending. Not every single mom can afford to take vacations every year or buy her kids designer clothes or shoes, computer games, CDs, and video collections. However, it is not unusual to see children of low-income single-parent families with these luxuries. Granted, some kids have a dad or other family members who buy these things, and some moms are great shoppers and find things at tremendous discounts. Yet many of these children get these things from moms who can't afford them but buy them to overcompensate.

Parents need to get over the idea that their children are suffering if they don't have the latest gadget or clothes. Many children of single parents grow up healthy and happy without them. Your perspective about your children's lack is what makes the difference.

One area that single moms struggle with is keeping up with the child's other parent. If you are struggling financially and your ex seems to be living carefree, it doesn't seem fair. You have to sacrifice when the person who is supposed to be helping you raise the children is living a more comfortable life. Many women see absent fathers starting new families and neglecting the old ones, or buying expensive gifts to win the children's affection instead of having a real relationship with them.

The struggle isn't really with what the other parent is doing or not doing; it is with your expectations of what he should be doing. Attitudes of envy or resentment will hurt you and your kids much more than your emotion will hurt the other parent. Studies have shown that bitterness will cause you illness and that your bitter attitudes are passed down to your children. It is not fair. You're right; life with only one parent is not fair to any child. Yet life is not fair, period. The sooner you and your children can accept what you can't change anyway, the better off you'll be. Learning to be the best mom you can be and to be content with what God has provided will take all your time and energy. God is the ultimate judge. He knows how to deal with your ex.

Codependency

This is a subject that has been covered by many good Christian authors, so I won't spend a lot of time on it. Codependency is a well-developed pattern of one person enabling another. My simplified explanation of enabling is doing something for someone else that they need to be doing themselves. Psychologists may balk at such a simple definition, but it helps me explain briefly how we become ingrained in our behaviors and expectations.

Codependency ingrained in families is hard to break. It affects your relationships with family, friends, co-workers, and even God. There are good Christian books and support groups available to help you discover whether or not codependency is a problem for you and to help you overcome it.

Balancing Relationships

We've established clearly that you need relationships to survive. Now the question is, how do I find the time for God, extended family, friends, and serving others?

We'll begin looking at answers in the next chapter, because you do need adult conversation and activity. It is not selfish to want to do grown-up things once in a while. You need adult input since you are doing the work of two people. Usually, the problem is that if you're spending most of your time with work, then your time with your children seems cut short. So you feel guilty if you leave them in order to have adult time.

It is a matter of setting priorities. You know these things are important, but you just don't have enough hours. But if you can "kill more than one bird with one stone" it is worth the effort. Single moms become great at economizing everything from money to time. The relationships you are developing meet two or three needs at one time. This should relieve some of the guilt. They are vital to your survival.

Were it not for the financial and spiritual help of my spiritual and genetic families, plus the great grace of God, I don't believe we would have made it. (Ellie; Medford, Oregon)

When you have your support system in place, then you will be strengthened for your journey. If you haven't tried to develop these relationships, then you can't blame the church, or family, or friends for not understanding you or your needs. It is your responsibility to begin working on these vital relationships, but the effort will pay off.

Four
Time Crunch: How to Fit It All In

Being a super-mom, super-provider, super-worker, super-friend, and super-Christian is time-consuming, not to mention tiring! You are not going to be great at everything; it is not possible. Just managing each day is enough to wear you out. The time element can bring pressures from all sides. Many of the respondents to my survey said that time management and balancing various demands of life are some of their greatest struggles.

Maintaining a home is time-consuming enough, and it is hard work. Yet single moms must handle all the cooking, cleaning, yardwork, repairs, shopping, laundry, and so on while being the primary breadwinner. Furthermore, they are still supposed to spend time with the children, be involved in activities at church or school, and maintain personal relationships with family and friends. Plus, if they are going to trust God, the relationship with him requires attention.

Most mothers want a more balanced life. In a recent poll of working mothers, 66 percent "would rather have more time with their children than money to spend on them." Forty-five percent, "have played hooky from work to be with their kids."

And 29 percent, "contemplate leaving their jobs at least once a month."[1]

Some of the working mothers polled were married. But the results show that it is a difficult balancing act for both single moms and married ones. Mothers are torn between providing for their kids and being with them. Doing it all, trying to be superwoman, can be exhausting.

Too Much to Do in Too Little Time

I know some super time managers. They are amazing. They clip coupons and feed three on less than forty dollars a week. One Saturday a month they cook all the family meals for the next four weeks. They pack nutritious lunches for the kids, they keep a clean house maintained by the whole family, and they volunteer at church and school. All this while holding down a full-time job.

I am a fairly organized person and used to do most of those things when I had a husband. Yet for most single moms it makes them tired just thinking about it.

Disaster Waiting to Happen

I don't know how your day goes, but I am freshly reminded of the struggle I had in parenting school-aged children when I observe a typical single mom's day. It goes something like this.

5:30 A.M.	Wake up; let out dog; feed dog
5:45 A.M.	Shower (pray while showering, no time to read the Bible)

6:00 A.M.	Start laundry; lay out younger children's clothes
6:15 A.M.	Wake up children; start getting them dressed
6:30 A.M.	Fix breakfast (Fast! Yell at kids to come to breakfast while taking out the trash)
6:40 A.M.	Tell kids to eat; you don't, you grab a glass of juice and head to the bathroom (kids turn on TV)
6:45 A.M.	Put on makeup and fix hair (yell at kids to turn off TV and finish breakfast)
7:10 A.M.	Tell kids to turn off TV and come in bathroom; everyone brushes teeth
7:15 A.M.	Tell kids to turn off TV and put on shoes while you dress
7:25 A.M.	Tell kids to turn off TV and put on shoes and get backpacks and put homework inside
7:28 A.M.	You turn off TV and watch school bus roll by
7:30 A.M.	Pack kids' and your lunches; drive kids to school
8:05 A.M.	Late for work again
10:30 A.M.	Call from school—child forgot important class project
12:00 NOON	Drive home on lunch break; pick up forgotten item; drive to school; drive back to work; eat sandwich on the way
2:30 P.M.	Children go to after-school program
5:00 P.M.	Boss tells you that you need to stay to complete a project
5:15 P.M.	Leave for after-school program; must be there by 6:00 P.M. or pay extra dollar per minute. Have to stop for bread and milk on the way

6:03 P.M.	Arrive at after-school program and pick up kids; pay three dollars for being late; talk about day on way home
6:15 P.M.	Kids have homework but try to convince you they need to play outside before dark
6:20 P.M.	You make kids change clothes; you change clothes; kids feed dog and start homework while you start dinner
7:00 P.M.	Sit down to dinner
7:20 P.M.	Kids clean up plates and go outside; you clean up kitchen; finish load of laundry started in the morning; skim through mail
7:45 P.M.	Call kids to come in for baths; pick up in living room; discover melted crayon on cushion
7:50 P.M.	Call kids again; start bath water
8:00 P.M.	Kids finally come in; start baths
8:30 P.M.	Story time and prayer with kids
9:00 P.M.	Lights out for kids; one kid comes out and says he needs poster board for tomorrow; you promise to buy it on way to school at twenty-four-hour store. Too late to do yardwork (already dark); too late to fix broken scooter or hang picture you've had since birthday (keep kids awake)
9:10 P.M.	Iron clothes for tomorrow; put laundry away; write checks for some bills; add to grocery list
11:00 P.M.	Collapse into bed (too tired to read Bible tonight, try again tomorrow)

As hectic as it is, this schedule can be disrupted by something as simple as spilled milk or a phone call. It can be disaster if the washing machine breaks or the toilet is stopped up, or if a child has an accident and needs immediate medical attention. In the single-mom household, there is no one to pass the baton to in this relay. You obviously have no time for outside interests. You've got to do it all. You've got to do it with a peaceful attitude. It is not easy.

Setting Priorities

I think every single-parent group should have one of the super time-manager moms give a talk on how to organize life. Task-oriented personalities will grab hold of the ideas and become very organized. However, people-oriented moms that are not task-oriented may be able to only apply one-third of what they hear, but even that much will benefit their family.

Time management boils down to setting priorities, simplifying your life, and establishing a flexible routine. You won't survive if you spend too much energy on any one priority. Your attitude about your priorities will influence how much time you'll spend on them. In the hectic world of single parenting, you have to choose wisely how you spend your time. Remember, balance is one of the greatest challenges for most single moms.

My primary partner in my journey is God, so that is my first priority. If I don't take time to get God's perspective on my day, then it is going to be a rough one.

The biggest mistake a single mom can make is to feel she does not have enough time for God. Having a special time each day to pray and read God's Word is the lifeblood of this single mom. I have made time for that by getting up an hour early and going to bed a half an hour later than the kids. I have seen God create time in my day in amazing ways. (Barbara; Bayfield, Colorado)

Work is a big priority, but it can also be the biggest investment of time. I have seen it over and over: Single moms working long hours to get ahead, traveling, leaving their children in the care of others or having latch-key children, working three jobs because one can't pay the bills. They barely see their children; they are exhausted; and they certainly don't have time for God. Most of them don't believe they have any choice.

Early on I made the mistake many single moms make in placing the highest importance on providing for my family. I didn't realize that God did not want that to be my highest priority. I had been taught early in my Christian walk that parents who didn't provide for their family were "worse than infidels," and I was pretty sure that that was bad. Like many single moms, I felt guilty for not being there for my children, but I believed that I had all this responsibility to bring home the paycheck.

Questions to Ask

Setting work priorities is complicated. Each situation is different. If you called me to ask whether or not you should take a new job, I would reply by asking several questions.

- Have you prayed about the job offer? Do you believe that this is a job God is guiding you to take?
- What would the job offer in benefits, time, or flexibility?
- What would you have to sacrifice to take the job? Will you still be able to parent your own children? Or will someone else do most of the parenting?
- What are you willing or able to sacrifice?
- What are your alternatives?

Some sacrifice may be necessary, but there is a limit. There is nothing wrong with taking a job to earn a better living. Yet there is something wrong with taking a job that would cause you to have others raise your children, or that would mean your children would become latch-key kids. If furthering your education to provide a better living for your children means they will suffer because Mom is stretched too thin between work, school, and home to be a good parent, then maybe schooling is not a good option for you right now.

It is easy to understand how low-income mothers feel the need to work long hours to get by, but this is not a problem limited to people with low incomes. Most of the mothers that responded to my survey made above $18,000 per year, and they struggled with having to give up precious time with their children to earn a living. The good news is that there are single moms who are not only surviving, they are thriving because they took a lesser job that had the flexibility that allowed them to be better parents and then learned to live within their incomes.

Your priority is to be a parent first, then you can focus on work or career. Your availability and support system should determine the extent of your work schedule. That doesn't give you a reason not to work, but it does give you cause to consider flexible options for work. Some people have lots of support from family and friends and thus have more flexibility. Many of the survey respondents said that they lived with relatives while they furthered their education or stabilized financially.

Where There's a Will

My daughter, Alicia, lives with me to further her education. She is the full-time mom to her son, Christian. I am not her built-in babysitter. I provide the home, we share in the household responsibilities, and she parents her son. I occasionally care for him and enjoy him on my terms. During the school year, Alicia has attended classes during Christian's school hours and then worked in the after-school program at his school. During the summer she has cared for other children to be able to stay home with him. It takes longer to get an education this way, but I admire her determination to be his parent first.

Alicia has learned to economize her time by combining two or three activities into one. Her job was selected not by pay scale but by the proximity it gave her to her son. Since she was the assistant director for the after-school program, she was actively involved in his after-school care and available to him at the same time. This job also allowed her to be off work on the same days Christian was out of school.

There are several single moms who said that they became schoolteachers for this same reason. This kind of time economy helps balance the work-family issue for single moms.

Economizing Time

Drive Time

In one job, which I had for two years, I had a forty-five-minute commute each way. Another job required a one hour, fifteen-minute drive each way, each day. I endured that long drive for only one year. I hated the boring driving time, but the jobs were worth it. Both of them were in a field I enjoyed and added to my confidence and creativity. Yet with such long commutes, I had little time for personal devotions, so I used this drive time to communicate with God. I listened to praise music on Christian radio or I just sang on my own and prayed. This time was wonderful and prepared me for work. Later, on the way home, I had the time to release everything and be ready for my family when I got there.

Whether your drive is ten minutes or an hour, you can use it to build your relationship with Christ. Some moms use the time they spend in the shower for prayer and praise or use the Bible for their reading material in the bathroom. It may not be traditional, but you can fit it in. As my relationship with Christ grew, I began to talk to him throughout the day, about everything. Today, I can't imagine lying down or getting up without prayer and praise.

Time for Yourself

Somewhere in your time economy, you have to have some time for yourself. It is not selfish to need devotional time, time with other adults, time to do something you enjoy, or just quiet time.

Parenting is your primary job, but you can't parent effectively without time away from the children. Use this time wisely. Some moms enjoy a movie with friends when their kids are away. Others just enjoy the quiet. Some get caught up on chores or errands. As long as this time does not detract from your parenting, you should enjoy it. If you don't have opportunities to spend time alone, then you need to build those relationships that we talked about earlier so that you can.

Don't allow your kids to be your sole reason for existence. Find some way to do something for yourself, even if it's small. Since I am a morning person, I get up early to have an hour or so for myself or take a bubble bath without interruption. I bowl once a week with some acquaintances because it is not being at work and not being at home and something I enjoy. (Debbie; Delta, Colorado)

Block out time for yourself just as if it were any other vital need. (Pamela; Suwanee, Georgia)

Time for the Home

There are several ways you can economize this time. One of the biggest mistakes moms make is to not involve the children in this area. Chores are good for children. They need to be taught personal responsibility for their own areas, and they need to contribute to the care of the family. Even very young children can help.

My children were toddlers when they began learning to put

their toys away. I had to supervise and not lose patience when they became distracted and wanted to play. The children discovered that the toys never danced their way into the toy box and that Mary Poppins and the toy fairy did not live at our house. Friends were also encouraged to help pick up toys before they went home. This simple skill is taught in most preschools, but it is sometimes neglected at home.

Depending upon the ages of your children, you can involve them with preparing for meals, cooking, cleaning, yardwork, and so on. Young children can learn to set a table. I came from a low-income family, but my mother made sure we kids knew how to set a table properly. She didn't teach us to cook, but that was because she wasn't very good at it and was never comfortable with sharing the kitchen. Nevertheless, table manners were very important and we all helped with cleanup after meals.

Getting kids involved with cleaning was pretty easy for me. Kids love spray bottles, so my children's first jobs were to clean all mirrors, furniture, and surfaces with spray cleaners. They usually used too much cleaner and at first I often had to wipe up after them, but they soon got the hang of it.

Another way to balance your time for home maintenance is to partner with another family. You can take turns fixing family meals and share them together. You can offer a skill that you have, such as sewing, hanging pictures or blinds, or painting walls in exchange for a skill that the husband in the family can do, such as cleaning gutters, tuning up the lawn mower, or putting heavy items in the attic. This isn't meant to be sexist. The idea is to exchange your skill for the skill you need. This economizes your time for friends and home.

I needed ceiling fans put in my house when I moved to Georgia. I asked a co-worker if he knew someone who could do the work and he said that he could. So I invited him, his wife, and his children over for an evening. The children played with my grandson, my daughter talked with my co-worker's wife, and I helped with his task. After the job was over we sat down to dinner.

Time to Serve

Although your time is precious, one area of time management should not be forsaken. In my work with low-income single parents, I hear of their needs and how the church did or did not help. Since these mothers know what it is like to be in need and have had to humble themselves to ask for help, they have great compassion for others in need. Those that have been helped have a great desire to return the favor by serving others. When I train churches to help single parents, I tell them to give the single parents opportunities to serve.

At first, I felt all I did was ask for help and give nothing back. But as time has gone by I've been asking less and have been given many opportunities to help others. (Lois; Arkansas City, Kansas)

> *Get involved in some kind of ministry at church (but not the singles ministry). By reaching out, I found that I was getting much more than I could ever give. Even though there are never enough hours in the day, make time to get involved at church. The people I met through serving were my lifeline during the difficult emotional times. (Kathleen; Jupiter, Florida)*

Most churches encourage single moms to serve by helping in the church nursery, as if that is the only place that they can serve. If your children are ministered to in the church nursery, then you should take a turn to serve, but do it only one time every other month. Don't feel guilty about not doing it more frequently. As an only parent you spend all week taking care of children all by yourself and you need adult fellowship when you're at church. There are numerous ways to serve in the church, and the nursery is just one of them. Look around at the various ministries in the church and see what else appeals to you. The idea is to find a place where you can offer a skill or talent and fill a real need.

> *Develop a servant's heart. Give to others. Share what you have. One Christmas Eve we went to the service at the local Gospel mission. We continue to give food and clothes. (Ellie; Medford, Oregon)*

Whenever possible, include your children when you serve. It is good for them to see that there are others who need help.

If your family is low-income, serving helps the children over-come the feeling that they are the "needy" family in the church. Other single-parent families serve because serving ful-fills a need to be used by God to help others. Your service should depend on your availability, personality, and gifting.

Find a volunteer activity to share with your children. You will have fun and come away with a sense of purpose and satisfaction. Some that we have enjoyed are building homes with Habitat for Humanity. Hosting a weekly kid's club for local chil-dren, including my own. Baking refreshments together for school or church activities. Manning a charity booth, taking a nursery shift together at church, collecting donations of clothing, or serving meals for a homeless shelter. (Susie; Arvin, California)

Again, you can economize your time with your children, with other adults, and with serving in one event or activity. This is how successful single moms manage to accomplish so much.

You only have twenty-four hours each day. You need to real-ize that you won't be able to do everything that needs to be done. Yet setting priorities and economizing your time will help you focus on what is really important.

Five
Parenthood Attitude: It's All in Your Head

The journey of single parenting is a long trip for some people and a short trip for others. Only God knows the length of this season of your life. The way for you to be really prepared for your survival is to prepare as though the journey will be long. If you are constantly thinking that this is just a phase, then you will put living on hold. That is not the way God wants you to live. It's not good for you and it's not good for your children.

Living in the past or living in the future causes unrest. Contentment only comes from being truly content in your present circumstances. For many of you, that means giving up on some preconceived ideas and expectations about this period in your life. One of your most important tools for survival is the right attitude. Your attitude affects every area of your life, including how you parent your children.

The Survival Attitude
This book is about surviving work as a single parent, but you can't work effectively if you are harboring the wrong attitudes.

These attitudes hinder your ability to see life from the right perspective.

For me, it was a matter of letting any preconceived notion about family and marriage die. I had to get to the place where I could accept that if it were supposed to be different it would be. I had to let go of the past and begin concentrating on what I was called to do in the present. That calling included being the best parent I could be. If I didn't get that part of my life in balance, then I wouldn't be able to balance work and family.

Letting Go of the Past

One of my greatest hindrances was my concept of family and marriage. It was fantasy. If the image did not die, I would be stuck, always looking for that prince on a white horse to come and save me. I would not fully live in the present.

Believe me, many women grieve more over the death of the fantasy than they do over the actual person that left. It was very hard to understand and accept that I didn't or couldn't have someone to love me. Eventually, I realized that at any time I could have had someone in my life, but the person may have been more of a detriment to my life than an asset. I had to find fulfillment elsewhere. For me, that fulfillment came in a relationship with a living God through his Son Jesus Christ.

When my husband left, I had a big hole in my heart. I missed being a couple. I'm still learning that God is the only "filler" for broken hearts. I knew it in my head, but didn't believe it in my heart, until time after time, God showed me I could trust him. (Mary; Mishawaka, Indiana)

One of the most effective ways of letting go is to forgive.

Learning to forgive helps you so much more than it does the person you are trying to forgive. It helps you to become content with your situation and accept it and embrace it. I struggled trying to forgive the woman my husband left us for. I just couldn't! I finally realized it was a choice to take captive my thoughts. Every time a negative thought would come into my head I would take it captive and tell myself out loud, "I choose not to think or feel this way." I asked the Lord to help me. (Tera; Mascoutah, Illinois)

Pray for your [ex]—it heals you. (Pegi; Claxton, Georgia)

Even if you [make mistakes], which you will, talk to God about it as you would talk to a friend, and get rid of it. Guilt is useless except for destroying your peace of mind and your ability to rest. (Kris; Kernville, California)

God wanted me to turn to him when I was lonely, afraid, or inadequate. I'm not saying it was easy. It was not. I struggled with it, just like you may be doing right now. At times, I still do. But I did find contentment. I came to understand that God really does have a plan for my life. That doesn't mean it will never include a husband, it just means that it doesn't include one right now. How do I know? Because I have not met a man who would positively enhance my life. Therefore, God's will for now is for me to remain single. If that changes, I'll know.

I find great comfort and confidence in looking at how God sees my life, and so can you. God is not surprised by your situation. He has confidence that you can be what he has designed you to be. And the great thing about it is that it doesn't all depend on you. I love what Philippians 1:6 says: "He who began a good work in you will carry it on to completion." It is God who starts the work of helping you change your perspective and, according to your cooperation, it is God who will give you what you need to change your life.

Focusing on the Present

Changing my perspective about my future allowed me the freedom to concentrate on what God was doing in the present.

People often ask me, "How do you know God's will for your life?" I used to think that was a deep, theological question that I couldn't possibly answer. In fact, I was so afraid of being out of God's will that I became debilitated. I knew that I had made many mistakes and must have missed God on many occasions. I would pray, but I was frustrated because I didn't "hear" an answer.

One of those times of frustration was when my children and I were living in my sister's home. I knew that I couldn't live there permanently and I earnestly needed God's wisdom about how to provide for my family. I tried to pray, but there were three adults and four kids in a very small house. That created a lot of activity and noise and I couldn't concentrate on praying. My sister walked by my room and did a double take when she saw me bowing my head and covering my ears. She stopped and asked me what I was doing.

"Trying to hear from God!" I cried.

"Well, don't you think that you could hear better if you took your fingers out of your ears?"

As humorous as her answer was, she spoke from the voice of experience. I was trying too hard to "hear" God. I was not mature enough in my Christian walk to understand that God led by his Word, by prompting, by confirming what to do, and by using other people. People describe this leading by saying that God speaks to the heart, not necessarily to the ears.

The Future Is in God's Hands
God isn't trying to hide his will from you. If your heart is right with him and you earnestly seek him, he will answer and give you wisdom. God knows you better than you know yourself. He knows how to get your attention. He knows how to get you where you need to be. All he needs is your willingness to follow his leading. A little self-examination will quickly determine if you are ready to do that:

- Are you withholding anything from God?
- Have you repented of anything you may have done to cause or worsen your situation?
- Are you holding any bitterness or unforgiveness against anyone?
- Are you willing to accept whatever God has for you?
- Have you decided to trust God?
- Are you ready and willing to acknowledge God's role in your life?

If you have honestly and completely released everything to God and have a right heart and a willing spirit, then you are in God's will. Even if you have strayed from his will, he knows how to get you back on track. Remember: he has a plan for your life. Your part is to go with God, not ask him to go with you. He leads, you follow. When you get that part down, you can move on to concentrating on what he wants to do in your life.

We have already established that your first role is to be a good parent. Since God entrusted you with children, you can be certain that his will is to help you care for those children. Where we get out of balance is when we think that we are supposed to be a provider first. God is the provider in your single-parent home. He also is the provider in two-parent homes. It was never supposed to entirely depend on you. Survival demands that you keep this perspective.

So many single moms put finding a mate, advancing their career, making money, involvement with church activities, meeting adult social needs, or any number of things first. Survival requires that you balance all the areas of your life. Your kids need you. You are their parent. Yet you need not be so absorbed in your children that you cannot work, socialize, dream, or do anything for yourself.

Trade Secrets

Single moms, like you, have learned some of these secrets of balancing family and work and raising balanced children. Since this is not a book on parenting, I'm going to share only a few tips that will help you balance family and work.

Through my own study and experiences I have come to realize that there are issues that are common among all parents. However, circumstances and the availability of support affect how a parent handles these issues.

Changing Your Parenting Perspective

Single parenting can come suddenly when there is a death, abandonment, or divorce. The normal family routine is abruptly interrupted. The grief of the parent often delays her dealing with the grief of the children. However, routine is one of the things in life that makes us feel normal and safe. The sooner you can establish a new routine in your home, the better.

Emphasize to your children that you are still a family even though there's no dad in the home. (Wanda; Ames, Iowa)

Try to keep your kids in as normal a lifestyle as possible. They need a schedule, friends, church, and a lot of love. At times I feel like my life is nothing but keeping up with the kids, but they deserve the best I can give them. My main focus is on them. (Lois; Arkansas City, Kansas)

Determine that your family will continue to be a family. Don't allow the lack of another parent in the home to keep you from establishing traditions. Don't try to let the children fill the role of the missing parent. Be the parent and let the children be the children.

Don't try to "fix" everything or provide everything for your kids. A lot of the problems they have they would have had in a two-parent household. (Dawn; Dothan, Alabama)

Let your children be children. Stop trying to grow them up so quickly. Never say to your child, you are just like your no-good daddy. I believe this phrase does great damage to the child emotionally (even if you don't see it at the time), mentally, and spiritually. If your children's father will not bring physical harm to you or them or purposely harm them emotionally, don't keep them apart. (Sonja; Jersey City, New Jersey)

Don't try to build close friendships with your children and allow them to view you as a friend and not a parent. Respect would be lost. Watch what you say when you are angry. Only date when God says this is the one. (Sandra; Duluth, Georgia)

Loving Your Child

For many parents, loving their children is easy. Yet many single parents have come from homes where they had poor role models and they don't know how to love their children.

Intense feelings of anger, abandonment, rejection, inadequacy, or resentment toward a missing mate can be transferred to a child. These feelings must be dealt with in professional counseling if you are ever going learn to love and provide your child with the foundation needed to succeed.

Children in single-parent homes often need reassurance that the remaining parent will not stop loving them and will not leave them. Let them know often that you are thinking of them.

Show your child affection and tell him or her that you love him or her at least once a day. If your child carries a lunch to school, include a note of encouragement. (Nancy; Saginaw, Michigan)

Let your children know that they are important to you.

Spend quality time with the children even if you have to sacrifice getting some chores done. Do things that your child likes, not just what you like. (Miriam; Stone Mountain, Georgia)

Child-Friendly Routine

The producer of the television program *Survivor* wrote a book on surviving and thriving in life. He states that he hopes he is a good parent to his two young children and that they understand that Dad has to be gone seven months out of the year for his work.

That is not thriving to me. That is work obsession. His wife is virtually a single mom who is raising his children seven months of the year alone. Does he really believe that the children are not going to resent that at some point in their lives? This perception of parenting is doomed to failure.

Children need their parent, not just his or her money. They know when they are important and when they are not. Work obsession is self-centered, not child-centered.

Being home when the kids are there in the evenings is crucial, if at all possible. Many moms are running to meetings and support groups to help satisfy their needs when the time would be better spent with their children. Try to maintain a positive "we are OK" attitude. It rubs off on the kids. And pray, pray, pray. (Pat; Ontario, Canada)

The time spent with the children should involve routine. So many moms are too exhausted to maintain a routine. Normal family life should be established as soon as possible. Involve the children in doing simple things that will help keep the flow smooth.

Don't pity your kids because you're single. Give [your children] tasks to do so they feel [like] an important family member. Reward them when there are tasks done well (at least verbally) and don't reward them when they're not. (Julie; Lockwood, Missouri)

> *I bought my children alarm clocks to help them learn how to get up to an alarm and become responsible. I occasionally put notes on their pillows, book bags, on their bedroom doors, telling them how much I love them and am proud of them. It makes the day special for them. (Michelle; Holton, Indiana)*

Nothing makes people feel more like family than a family meal. This is a good time to catch up with each other after spending the day apart.

> *Always make a meal and make all the kids sit down for dinner, and pray. (FranHoise; Alma, Arizona)*

Teaching Godly Principles

The primary example our children see of God's love is shown in how we parent. It is hard to accept a loving Father God if a child doesn't see unconditional love at home. While raising my children, I prayed fervently that God would help me be the kind of parent he wanted me to be. Part of being a godly parent is praying for your kids. You need to daily pray for their health and safety. Pray that God will give them favor. Thank God daily for them. You may even pray for their future mates. Yet don't just pray for or about your children. Pray with them. Let them hear you pray. Let them see you reading the Bible. Read the Bible with them. Share some victories from your own Christian walk with them.

Pray with your children about specific issues, then talk about the answers when they come. (Gail; Virginia Beach, Virginia)

Let your children know when things are difficult for you. Tell them you are praying about your struggles and ask them to pray for you because you KNOW it will make a difference. (Paulette; Mobile, Alabama)

When you ask your children to pray for you, make sure you don't burden them with the details of your struggle. Just ask them to pray about a specific but nonthreatening request. But don't give them more than they can handle or allow them to take on the responsibility for your situation or happiness.

Try not to treat any of the kids as an adult. Don't burden them with problems that only an adult should or could handle. Let them enjoy their childhood as much as they possibly can. (Marie; Melbourne Beach, Florida)

Don't expect boys to be the man of the house. Just remember, it is not their fault you are single. Just love the kids and be there always for them. (Nanette; Winder, Georgia)

Discipline

Being a good parent takes time and energy—things that are in short supply for single moms. One of the areas that may suffer when a parent is busy juggling multiple responsibilities designed for two parents is the area of discipline. Experts say that consistency and keeping a calm perspective are the most important aspects of discipline.

When you're tired, you may ignore a child's behavior or snap over situations that require firm discipline. You may be tempted to belittle your children. Some parents think this makes children tougher to be able to handle name-calling at school. Children are resilient, but their spirits can be crushed when they are demeaned by a parent from whom they so desperately want approval. Providing consistent love and approval along with discipline brings balance to the family. One single mom has taped on her computer Ephesians 6:4. ("Do not provoke your children to anger, but bring them up in the discipline and instruction of the Lord.") She says her son has a temper, and she had to learn the hard way that disciplining him in an angry way backfires! Pay attention to how your children respond to your discipline.

Follow through with discipline and be consistent. It's hard because you're tired, have worked all day, can't take another minute, etc., but I promise it will pay off. I prayed and asked God to help me instill in my children his principles and his heart. (Jean; city unknown)

> *Do discipline. Do be honest; do keep the doors of honest communication open. Do take your children to God in prayer and seek his leading. Do seek godly role models. Do rear your children by the Word of God. (Sherial; Dayton, Texas)*

Remember the old adage of counting to ten before you respond? Well, it works, but instead of just counting, try praying. I discovered how effective this was when my children hit the teen years. Teens have a way of expressing attitudes that can cause overreactions in weary parents. There came several points where my style of discipline no longer worked and had to change as my children changed. In frustration, I found myself reacting instead of acting on their behalf. I had to learn to stop and pray when that feeling of reacting started. When I did this, God gave me the strength and perspective to handle the situation properly.

When you find yourself reacting, remember, it is not your child's fault that you are tired. He or she can wait a minute or five, until you have the perspective and strength you need to deal with the situation. Prayer is better than counting to ten because when you take your request to God he provides what you need to handle it.

Perspective on the Absent Parent

Abandoned parents, those who have been hurt in the breakup of a relationship, or those who still have to deal with a substance or emotional abuser may have a hard time maintaining the right perspective about the absent parent. Experienced moms discover that if they keep their attitudes in check it helps their children.

Safety Issues

If there is a real danger that the absent parent may cause harm to you or your children, then seek the court's protection for your family. If there is no real threat then it is best for the children if they can remain involved with the absent parent. Noncustodial parents who are involved with their children are more likely to pay child support. The children are more secure. To assist the children in this relationship requires that you keep your wounds and ill feelings to yourself.

Never speak negatively of your ex in front of your kids. (Jennifer; Johnson City, New York)

Keep a good working relationship with your children's father. This will avoid unnecessary conflicts with visitation and the overall upbringing of the children. (Portlynn; Atlanta, Georgia)

In some cases the absent parent is not a threat but instead is a poor role model for your children. He may not keep promises to the children or may not keep regular contact. How the children deal with this relies heavily on your response. Most mothers get angry and try to stop all involvement. Some overcompensate by spoiling the children. Others attempt to remedy the situation by trying to go out and replace the parent with a better model.

Try not to worry and above all try not to blame yourself for every little thing that you feel the children are missing out on. Don't rush out and feel that you have to find a partner because life is rougher than you are used to. My children laugh, but I explained to them that if God means for me to have a husband in my life, he'll have to direct me with a neon sign. Give your children the time they need to adjust to this new lifestyle. (Sheila; Downers Grove, Illinois)

Don't feel sorry for your children because their father is not there. God will be their father and he is the best there is. Don't try to be both father and mother to your children. For whatever reason, only God knows, being without a father in the home is just one of the crosses your children will have to bear. Pampering, babying, or feeling sorry for their misfortune will not make things better for your children. Actually, treating them like that will make things worse. God has great plans for them, as he does for all his children (yourself included). I believe this kind of attitude will help the children accept their life without a father more readily. (Lori; Vancouver, Washington)

Against the advice even given by the church, I chose not to be involved in dating and relationships and devoted myself to my children. What your children see in you and how they live now is what is the foundation for their future. What they will become is happening today. (Ellie; Medford, Oregon)

Mentoring

A father is important to both boys and girls. When the father is not available or is available only on a limited basis, kids tend to suffer. Involving your children with two-parent families is one way for them to have the model of good fathering. Another way is to involve them in activities that include men. This is so important because studies show that we develop our first relationship with God based upon our relationship with our fathers. If we don't have godly modeling, we are going to have a distorted view of "Father God." As they grow, children learn that natural fathers aren't perfect, and they learn that God loves on a different level, but initially, they only know the model they have seen.

Find men in your church who can mentor your boys, teach them life skills, and help their spiritual walk. (Jennifer; Johnson City, New York)

> *Raising your child in church gives him the faith to believe that he will never be without a father because he has God. (Antonitta; Atlanta, Georgia)*

I often hear from single moms that struggle with finding godly mentors. I know that God hears their pleas. I firmly believe that he handles each child differently. I struggled and begged for mentors for my son, David. For a year or two he had some mentors when he was in a Christian scouting-type program. I sent him to boys' camp in summers and to the youth group at church, but I didn't see anyone personally involving himself in David's life. My son's father, when he was around, was not a good role model. After the divorce my son had no contact with his father. This caused me to be concerned about my son's perception of men and of God. I worried about it all through his teen years because I wasn't aware of how God was working in his life. God provided what he needed; I just didn't know it until years later.

For instance, one pastor made a big impact on David. Small things mean much more than we can imagine. This pastor was always sensitive to my son, but at one service, he decided he would bless my son as a father would his own son. That simple prayer was so moving that it brought my son to tears. Seeing my son moved touched me and I cried. When we moved five hundred miles away and my son decided to marry, he asked that pastor to perform the ceremony. The pastor agreed and prayed for my son and his wife again during the ceremony. The prayer was such a blessing that my son and I cried again, and so did my daughter and my new daughter-in-law.

Just as God can handle being a husband and father to you, he can handle fathering your child. Just trust him. Trusting God to help you parent and to be the missing parent in your child's life allows you to deal with the other areas in your life that you have to balance.

Parenting Resources

When my children were young, there were very few resources to help me parent alone. Today there are more materials available.

Christian organizations such as Focus on the Family have an abundance of resources on the issue of parenting and a special edition of *Focus on the Family* magazine just for single-parent families.[1] There are many other good Christian authors who have addressed the subject of parenting. If you can't afford to purchase a certain book or videotape, check local public or church libraries. If what you seek is not available there, ask if they can get it for you.

Read everything James Dobson has to say on parenting. Chuck Swindoll has a great book [too]. It is biblically based child rearing. Read and apply! (Julie; Lockwood, Missouri)

If your church doesn't have a single-parent support group where you can discuss the issues of parenting children alone, see if you can get one started. There are two national evangelical organizations that have training and a curriculum for churches that want to start single-parent family ministries: Barbara Schiller's Single Parent Family Resources, and Theresa McKenna's Single Parent Family Ministry Resource Center.[2]

Parenting is such an integral part of the single-parent life. If this area is not in balance then all other areas will suffer. It's not impossible. God has entrusted your children to you, and he will help you be the kind of parent you need to be. This is a prerequisite to equipping yourself for work.

Six
Work Conditioning:
Getting in Shape for the Workplace

Balancing the responsibilities of home and family is a big enough job, but you must also manage to survive the workplace. The mistake many people make is to not prepare properly. Knowing your obstacles is only part of the preparation. When the other areas of your life are in balance, and you pull together the right equipment for your particular journey, you will be prepared to come out in good shape at the end of the adventure.

Have you ever experienced the self-respect, self-confidence, and healthy independence that come when you tackle a difficult task for which you have carefully and patiently prepared?[1]

Original Equipment

God has equipped you to survive. He has prepared you with some specific equipment designed to fulfill his plan for your life. This equipment includes a distinct personality and a propensity for certain types of activity. The problem is that many struggling single parents are too busy to stop and discover what that equipment is, or their talents get buried or misdirected through life experiences. It is vital to your survival to know what God has already given you.

In addition, your true sense of self may be distorted if you have lived in a family with drug or alcohol abuse, physical, verbal, emotional, or sexual abuse, or poverty or neglect. Adapting to stressful family environments means taking on roles that you may not have been designed to play. In fact, some people are so good at their adapted roles that they become completely unaware of who they are. They no longer recognize themselves.

Whatever your past, what God has placed in you is still there. There is a tendency in Christianity to downplay strengths—acknowledging them might be considered prideful, or they might be judged unacceptable for women. Yet looking at your strengths is not pride. These are your God-given tools for survival. Now is the time to stop and rediscover what God has given you.

Begin to remember who you are. Before marriage, children, and career, you were your own person. Reach for who you remember being and expand on it. Start small, one step at a time and accomplish a small task, goal, dream you have longed for. Through your personal discovery you begin to find your way through the trees. (Jaide; Arlington, Texas)

Personality, Propensity

As we have already discussed, God has equipped us from birth with the basic skills and abilities we need to survive. Yet these talents often get buried or misdirected through life experiences. It is vital to your survival to know what God has already put in you. There are several good personality assessment tools[2] available in the Christian marketplace to help you discover your individual makeup. The tests are easy to take and usually pretty accurate. If you cannot afford a test, this would be a good reason to approach your church for help. When you have found out how God wired you, you will have a clearer picture of God's direction for your life.

I took a personality test when I hired on at Crown Financial Ministries, but I was so out of touch with my true personality that I thought the test was wrong. I still didn't really know myself thirteen years after my divorce. I took that test several times and still thought I must be taking it incorrectly because I kept getting the same results. I finally went to my children and siblings. They all agreed the test was accurate.

What the test revealed as my strengths I saw as my weaknesses. All the things that I was punished for as a child were the negative side of my strengths. That stubbornness that was so obvious when I was a child was the negative side of determination. The demand to be heard became influence. I still have to be careful that I don't fall into the weaknesses of those strengths, but I was amazed—God created me this way for a reason!

You, too, have a unique personality and God-given talents. God created you the way you are for a purpose. The strengths that he placed in you will equip you for his plan. It may be that he has equipped you to be out in front of others as a leader. It may be that God has equipped you to be a support person providing invaluable encouragement and help to the leaders. Each person's contribution of talents is important. God has a certain role that only you are equipped to play. If you are out of touch with the person God created you to be, there are several ways to begin your personal discovery. The most significant way is through prayer.

Sit in a quiet place and think back over your entire life. Examine who you think you are. Consider what others tell you about yourself.

What were you like as a child? What did your parents say about you, good and bad? Don't ignore what you think could be described as a negative characteristic, since it may be the flip side of a wonderful strength.

Finally, consider what God says about you. He says that you are "fearfully and wonderfully made" (Psalm 139:14). He created you for a purpose. You are designed to succeed when you follow his plan.

Some people are more task-driven than people-oriented. People who are naturally task-oriented thrive when they can accomplish a task. Those who are people-oriented feel stifled and unfulfilled if they aren't able to interact with people.

Your personality greatly affects how you relate to your family, friends, boss, co-workers, and your work in general. There are analytical people who figure out solutions to complex problems. Some people are bold leaders who have strong opinions about how things should be done. They are visionaries who see the big picture and inspire others. These leaders are greatly needed, but others are perfectly happy being in the background providing support.

Knowing how you are oriented is very important to your success in the workplace. Being in the wrong job can cause much stress. You may be able to do the job. You may even be able to do it well. But doing a job that you are equipped to do brings much more peace and satisfaction.

Another part of your unique design is your propensity for certain activities. Some people like physical jobs that have them outdoors or working with their hands. Other people like creative thinking or problem solving and are into the details. Thank God that many people have a need to be supporting of or caring for people.

Propensity thus is not the skills you have developed along the way; it is your inborn drive or tendency to function in a certain way.

Skills, Talents, Abilities

Although your personality and propensity are set at birth, specific interests, abilities, and skills are developed over time. Sometimes you develop skills that have little in common with your personality and propensity because you have had to adapt to certain conditions.

I have worked some jobs that were very clearly not in line with my personality or propensity. For example, I was working for a fire coat manufacturer as an entry-level customer service representative when I was faced with a layoff. I was given the option of staying employed by taking a job in data entry. I had never operated a computer before. In addition, I discovered very quickly that I was not a steady, routine type of person. I needed creativity and variety, but this job was my only choice at the time.

This position often brought me to the point of frustration and tears. I had a boss who cursed and slammed down phones. He was not a believer, and I struggled between being afraid of him and wanting to tell him off. I spent every lunch hour in prayer and searching the Bible for the strength to go back to work. I wanted to be delivered from the job. God did answer me, but not by removing me from the job. He gave me the strength to keep quiet and a way to make the job more challenging.

I barely knew how to type when I took the job. My trainer, the departing employee, was a very good instructor. She told me that accuracy was more important than speed. That was good news because I was very slow. She sent about five hundred requisitions for fire coats to the plant each week. I started by sending two hundred per week, but they were accurate.

I know that the only reason I was able to keep that job in the beginning was because God wanted me there. I was determined to learn whatever I had to learn as quickly as possible so that I could be delivered as soon as possible.

After meeting my accuracy goal, my second challenge was matching the quantity of requisitions the former employee had sent to the plant each week. I met that goal after about six months. My final challenge was to consistently beat all previous records. The second year, I did that. While working only three days per week in order to attend full-time college classes, I consistently sent seven hundred to eight hundred requisitions per week and sometimes sent over one thousand. I came in at 6:00 A.M. in order to have faster access on the computer terminal.

During those times in prayer, God led me to pursue a

career in Christian broadcasting. I continued to work for the company while taking college-level courses, but I spoke often of my desire to work in Christian television. After two years, God opened the door for me to take a position as assistant to the development director at a local Christian television station. The move was a wonderful testimony to my co-workers at the manufacturing company. Yet during those two years, I had learned some very definite things about work and about myself.

That job had been my first full-time job since becoming a single parent. I knew nothing about working in an office environment and I quickly discovered what I did not like to do. I learned about my need for challenge, variety, and accomplishment. I learned how to make routine tasks interesting for me. By the time I left the position, I actually liked it.

Yet the best part was this: before I left, my difficult boss called me into his office to ask me if I was a Christian. When I answered that I was, he said he had never met a Christian who really lived what they believed until he met me.

The Process of Discovery

Begin With Yourself

To begin exploring your skills, talents, and interests, consider what you naturally do well. Look at some of the abilities required for jobs that you have had. Ask yourself:

- What jobs have you enjoyed?
- What types of activity are most important to you?
- Do you like being outdoors or do you prefer being indoors?

- Do you enjoy physical labor or thinking and creating?
- Do you enjoy interacting with people more than accomplishing a task?
- Do you get stressed out over organization or is it a pleasure to put something in order?
- Are you a natural problem solver?
- Would you rather be more of a behind-the-scenes support person or would you like to be the boss?

Look for hidden skills in jobs that you have done but didn't enjoy, such as things that were necessary for you to learn in order to fulfill your responsibilities. Also look at activities you learned that you definitely do not enjoy.

Make Time to Volunteer

Another way to discover talents, skills, and interests is to volunteer. Yes, I said volunteer. We have already discussed your lack of time and financial restraints. Yet we have also discussed your need to be involved in serving others. This is another way to economize time. If you are creative in where you volunteer, you can use this time to uncover a new interest, skill, or ability that will help you in your direction for work.

When I ask at seminars, "Where is the first place single parents are asked to volunteer in the church?" the answer is always the nursery. As we have discussed, if your children benefit from the nursery, then you should take your turn in serving there. Yet single moms have the full responsibility for caring for their children. They need a break and adult socialization. Unless you absolutely adore children, you shouldn't volunteer your time for nursery duty more than once every other month or once per quarter. That is enough time to learn whether or not caring for children should be your career direction.

As mentioned, there are numerous places in the church to serve. Maybe you have an untapped creative side that you can explore by volunteering to work with music, choir, or drama, or helping with church newsletters. Explore your organizational skills by starting a single-parent group or helping the church with special events. Explore your serving skills by being a greeter, visiting the sick, helping the needy, or working in benevolence. Test your physical skills by working on the construction team. Try your teaching skills by leading a Sunday school class or doing a workshop on an area of interest. Investigate your skills at details by helping the accounting department count offerings and prepare reports, or become a volunteer budget counselor to help members establish budgets.

Many of these and other opportunities exist in most churches. Some volunteer activities can be done from home, while others require going out or being at church. The goal should be to try different volunteer positions until you find one that fits and can lead to a direction in employment. Be sure to include these discovered skills in your résumé.

Explore a Field

If you have an idea about what type of work you would enjoy, begin investigating that field. Network with friends, church members, and family to find someone who is doing the type of work you are interested in pursuing. Visit or interview the person to find out what type of starting positions may be available so you can investigate the work up close. Working in or near the field can confirm your direction positively or negatively.

My daughter Alicia's childhood dream was to be a doctor to children. She was an excellent student and had the passion for it. This was her goal and she refused to let single parenting interfere with it. When she became the primary provider for her son, she determined to set a short-term goal to complete an eighteen-month course on medical assisting to further investigate the medical field from a staff position. She worked in a variety of doctors' offices, including pediatric offices.

After observing the medical field for two years, she decided that she no longer wanted to be a medical doctor. The limitations set on medical doctors would inhibit the relationship that she wanted to have in caring for children. It was a very difficult conclusion, since she had dreamed about being a doctor her whole life. She refused to base the decision on the fact that she was a single parent. Single parents can and do become excellent doctors. Her decision was based on whether it was the right position for her.

Alicia's people orientation and desire to care for children were part of her God-given makeup. Her personality and propensity did not change when she decided to leave medicine. She made the decision to continue her education. She still desires to work with children, but now she has focused her education more in the area of child psychology, with the goal of working as a school psychologist or counselor. This career will allow her the flexibility to work in harmony with her own child's school schedule.

Network, Network, Network

It is not easy to break into some fields without education or training. Yet most companies have starting positions that allow you to observe the field of interest. It helps if you know someone in the field or business to give you a referral. If you don't know someone in the field you are pursuing you may be able to network to find that person. Your church is a great place to network. The people you know may know someone you can contact. That is how I landed my dream job.

I didn't really know what I wanted to do until I was facing that dreaded data entry job in 1985. When I discovered my desire for Christian broadcasting, I didn't know anyone in that field. However, my sister knew someone at church who worked at the local Christian television station. She introduced us and we discussed several ideas. To my surprise, the man—an executive at the station—asked me to submit my ideas to him so the staff could consider them. This connection to the right person was a God thing, but it required certain steps from me. I had to let my interest be known among my friends and acquaintances, and I had to pursue the contact that was given to me. It took two more years from the time I met the man until I landed a job at the station. We had sporadic contact over that time. When an entry-level job in my desired field opened, he knew who I was and of my interest.

Some first jobs, such as clerk or assistant, usually don't require formal education or a great deal of training, but they may require some experience. Other jobs may require some education or training. If you are still on the investigating side of your career, these jobs may be the best route for you to explore your interest in that field. Inexpensive ways to obtain experience include volunteer work, attending classes at a local community college, or developing skills in a temporary job office.

Consider Further Education

You may already have a field in mind, but you may be hindered because the position requires the college education you don't have. If you are already certain that the career for you is a professional position, then you need to explore your educational opportunities.

If you are working the entry-level job to explore the field, you can take a few classes of interest on the side. Students who take less than half-time credit hours for a quarter or semester may be able to apply for scholarships, but they usually do not qualify for grants. However, many companies have education reimbursement plans for people who intend to stay with the company and use their skills there.

Grants and scholarships are based on various criteria. They may be available to low-income families, high achievers, and to people who are pursuing particular fields or have met certain conditions. You can begin researching grant and scholarship opportunities at a local community college or library. If this is what you believe that God wants for you, then go for it.

Get a college education as soon as you are widowed or divorced. (I was widowed at age twenty-four.) Do not rely on public aid or Social Security survivors' benefits. This income will come to an end when your child is sixteen. Focus on college, not public aid. (Anna; Mount Vernon, Illinois)

Living with parents, friends, or other relatives can be a tremendous help in furthering your education. Your expenses will be low, so you can put more money toward your education without accumulating debt, and you will have more time for your child if you are sharing household responsibilities with others.

There are many ways to go to school with minimum debt. After two years of university (of course living modestly) I owed about $3,000, which I paid off within sixteen months. My greatest challenge was to get through school while also being a full-time mom. I put my time with God and my daughter first and when able I chose to work close by, instead of spending a lot of time on the road traveling. I have adapted to making less money, live modestly, and [I'm] here at home as much as possible. (Mirta; Summerville, South Carolina)

If you aren't able or don't believe you need to further your education to meet your goals, your priority should be finding work with flexibility and benefits that allow you to be a parent first. That doesn't give you the out to not work. That just means you need to be selective in what you do. Some employers are favorable to families. Others become more favorable after you are a proven worker.

Assess Life Skills

To complete your assessment you need to include the skills, talents, and abilities that you have developed in the course of your life. These are valuable tools, not to be taken lightly.

Single moms gain experience in organization, first aid, caring for children, mentoring, teaching, delegating, cooking, cleaning, some repairing, judging, refereeing, coaching, and numerous other skills. Some of these are really well developed. You may have had to face situations you didn't think you could face. You have had to find strength and confidence that you didn't know that you had. You have had to rely on God for more than you ever imagined. These experiences are essential survival tools that can be included in your résumé.

Developing a Career Goal

Now that you know a little more about your personality, propensities, skills, and experience, you should have a good idea what will be needed for your career choice. Now it is time to develop a plan. The first step in any plan is to write it down. It is a simple procedure, but one that many people miss. I have prepared some questions that will help you begin the process.

- What natural or developed skills have you acquired at work or at home?
- What experience in life, work, home, or volunteering do you have in using those skills?
- What interests you?
- What are your inborn or developed talents?
- What kind of job might you want to pursue, including your dream job?

- What are the hindrances to working in any of those jobs?
- What people do you know in those fields?
- Who have you talked to about those fields?
- What are potential starting positions in those fields?

Use the information you have gathered to begin writing your résumé. If you don't know how to write a résumé, ask around to find someone who can help you. When your résumé is ready, you can begin applying for that starting position in your field of interest.

After you have investigated one field of interest and determined your direction for that field, you will need to take the next step in developing your plan. This next step may include investigating opportunities for advancement, additional education or training, or another field. This process will be short for some people, but may take years for others, depending on the results of your investigation and your final career goal.

Finding your career direction can become discouraging at times. This is when survival is hard. But you can learn to survive the process and eventually thrive.

Don't be too hard on yourself. Don't try to figure out your new life too quickly—it's going to take a lot longer than you might imagine to figure out a workable routine for yourself and your kids. Be willing to make lots of mistakes, as you discover what doesn't work. Single moms are often so overwhelmed that we don't appreciate the daily miracles. (Lisa; Parkville, Maryland)

For your plan to succeed, it must line up with God's plan. If you have prepared properly you should have some idea what that is. If you have God in your life, you have a secret weapon. You have something that sets you apart from others. You have his leading, his preparation, and his favor. Your plan must be flexible enough to include what God may be doing with your life.

Seven
Work Survival: Putting It All Into Practice

Have you ever taken a trip and thought that you were prepared, only to find out that you were not? My mother took my older sister and me on our first and only family vacation after my father's death.

We were going to Nashville from Dayton, Ohio, not a long trip. Depending upon stops, it normally was five to six hours. Mom grabbed some maps, gathered us up, gassed up the old car, and headed out.

Our trip took longer than expected because Mom was an adventurous and spontaneous person who decided to take some side trips along the way. By the time we reached Tennessee it was dark and we were still on a country road. It seemed to go on forever. The only light came from our headlights. My sister and I were hanging on to each other, begging Mom to find the highway again. Then, suddenly, a cow showed up in our headlights. Mom slammed on the brakes. We didn't hit the cow, thank goodness, but now we were stalled in the middle of a very dark country road. My sister and I were terrified. Mom calmly restarted the car and went on down the road. Five miles later we found a gas station, where she asked for directions to the highway. We made it to Nashville, but it was the middle of the night.

A Light on the Path

I look back on that trip and realize a few things. Mom could have done things to be more prepared. Starting earlier in the day would have allowed time for spontaneity and would have gotten us to Nashville during daylight. Another thing: sitting in that stalled car was scary because all we could see around us was darkness. Not knowing how far we were from help caused us much concern. Keeping our eyes on the light on the road instead of looking around at the darkness would have prevented much of the fear. We never know how close the end of the journey is and, although we may not realize it at the time, God is with us.

I love the fact that God calls himself I AM. He is there when and where you need him. He has a plan for your life and he is in control of that plan, but his Word says that he is a light unto our path. Like the headlights of our car, his illumination is right in front of you. If you look behind or too far ahead, there may be darkness and fear, but you will have what you need in the present if you keep focused on the lighted path.

One interesting thing about a journey: it always has a beginning and an ending. All things will come to an end. What a relief when my mother, sister, and I found light and direction. It was always there. We were closer than we thought, but we couldn't see it. God knew that it was there, but we had to trust that it was there. Your single-parent experience is a journey and it will end. How you experience the journey is up to you.

If God has a plan then he must have a way to accomplish that plan, which usually involves active participation from the individuals involved. You may be immobilized because of fear or because you believe that if God has a plan then all you have to do is sit and wait on him to perform his miracles. You may be too consumed by life to even think about God's role. Or you may be taking things into your own hands because you believe that God has placed all the responsibility for the plan on you and you have to figure it out.

However, if you honestly believe that God is in control of the plan, you will be actively seeking it. There is a certain amount of rest and comfort knowing that he is playing the primary part and your part is secondary.

Flourishing in the Workplace

Mary Welchel, author and host of a radio program for Christian working women,[1] speaks and writes on the subject of how a Christian woman should function in the workplace. Other wonderful Christian authors have also explored the area of Christians in the workplace. Rather than duplicate here what is already available, I suggest that you look for these resources at your local Christian bookstore or library. I will share with you some of the more common themes that are necessary for your single-parent journey.

God, Our Employer

The Bible tells us to work "as unto the Lord." That means that when we are at work or talking about work, we should be behaving as though God were our employer. This should be our attitude whether we work in a Christian or a non-Christian workplace.

Some Christians believe that working in a Christian workplace would be so much easier than dealing with the attitudes and behaviors of non-Christians. It is nice not to hear dirty jokes or cursing or tales of someone's sexual life. However, you are going to encounter personality differences in every workplace. Bosses can sometimes seem unfair even in Christian ministries. Inappropriate behavior can take place in any work environment. None of this diminishes your responsibility to work as unto the Lord.

Your attitudes are expressed in your behavior at work. Some people hate being known as the Christian at work because they feel such pressure to be perfect. You don't have to be perfect, but you do have to present the right attitude to your boss, your co-workers, and your customers.

Personalities play a large part in how you will get along with others. Some people like to be in control and don't like to have that control challenged. Others want a free flow of ideas. Some like detail but are not people-oriented. Some like people and don't want to be bothered with details. The best way to discover how to work with each boss or co-worker is to observe how they interact with others. Consider their motivation. Work with their personalities. But don't allow personality to become an excuse not to deal with important issues.

Perspective About Your Boss

You may be thinking at this point, "But you don't know my boss!" That's true, but God places all authority. And if God places or allows all authority, then he knows who your boss is and he has permitted him or her to be in that position of authority. Your role is to respect the position, even when you don't respect the boss. God is your ultimate boss. As your boss, he places certain people in authority over you. You have a responsibility to submit to that authority until God removes you from that employment. The only time you should not submit to that authority is when your boss requires that you do something that is a sin against God.

There was a time that I did not understand this concept and struggled with a boss in a Christian environment. As a single mom, I struggled between work and being home with my children. I was working in my dream job in Christian television, but my children were acting out. They were in their early teens and were latch-key kids. A new boss came to work for the company. He was intense, young, married, and had no children. We didn't agree on much.

Our differences exploded when I took a personal day to deal with my daughter. Although I felt justified and argued to the point of tears, I was let go. It was going to happen anyway because the company was facing layoffs, but mine happened sooner because of my conflict with the boss.

I argued with God about it for six months. I knew that I was right. My kids came first. Why did that man get to stay while I was out of my dream job? Jobs were hard to get and my background in broadcasting did not open up many opportunities. I worked temporary jobs when I could get them. I prayed. I cried. I tried to start my own business, which failed. I tried to pay my bills, but couldn't. I knew that God could rescue me, but he chose not to. I didn't understand. I wanted to work. Was this God's will?

Provision Attitude

I learned so much during those months after the layoff. I eventually realized that God does place all authority. I learned that God would argue my case if I would let him. Eventually, I accepted my part in the fiasco with the boss. Later, his boss unexpectedly apologized to me for how I was treated and for having to lay me off. I learned that God was my provider. Also, I found out what God already knew: that my children needed me at that time much more than I needed a paycheck.

I was certain that the world would fall apart if I didn't work full time. It didn't. Yes, I faced terrible financial pressures, but creditors couldn't take what I didn't have. We ate every day. We did without electricity for two weeks in the summer, but it didn't hurt us. I didn't even lose our rental home. After two years of this, I ended up owing my landlord almost $5,000 in past rent. He was not a Christian and he didn't know why, but he could not evict us. I eventually paid off all my debts, some miraculously, and paid my landlord back by doing repairs and improvements to his house. The best part is that I later did freelance camera work for the new boss who had caused me so much grief. We worked very well together.

It is sometimes difficult to see God's attitude when you're in the midst of the struggle. God did not perform the way I thought he should. He did not provide "manna from heaven." He did not send a rescuer in the form of a new husband. He did not give me the full-time job that I believed he should. When God says his ways are not our ways, he means it. Trust means accepting and believing that God has a plan, he is working, and we don't always know what it is.

Dress Attitude

Since we are working for the Lord, we need to make the best impression we can. And that includes appearance. Dress for success. A cliché, yes, but nonetheless important. Promotion comes from the Lord, but you have to be prepared for it. Employers are more likely to advance workers who are a cut above the rest.

Dress codes have loosened tremendously over the last few years. Many corporate offices are now "dress casual" every day. Some manufacturing offices allow very casual attire, such as jeans and T-shirts. This relaxed atmosphere is supposed to help workers feel more comfortable and, consequently, get more work done.

Now that workplaces have fewer standards for employees, more and more Christian women are giving in to the society norms with short or high-slit skirts, tight clothing, or revealing blouses. Others are giving in to extreme hairstyles, tattoos, or body piercing.

Successful workers always are professionally groomed. I am all for comfort but I am also for presenting a professional appearance. If your ultimate employer is God, then you need to meet or exceed all the expectations for dress in the workplace. That doesn't mean you can't wear khakis if that is the dress code; it means that the slacks should be cleaned and pressed and paired with a nice shirt or jacket.

Dress as well as you can afford to dress for work. If you can only afford two new outfits per year, make sure they are classic ones that make you look polished and don't go out of style. There are inexpensive ways to dress well. You can often find good work clothes at consignment stores. You can help yourself and other single parents by asking professional women in the church to donate gently worn clothing for women in need.

The Right Habits

When considering an employee for promotion, another area of scrutiny is work habits. A good worker gets to work on time, works when scheduled to work, only calls in sick when she or her child is really sick, and gives her best to get the job done. If you are struggling in any of these areas, you need to look at why these are a problem for you.

Starting the Workday Right

Getting to work on time can be a challenge for single moms, but many do it every workday. Unless you have chosen a job with an impossible work schedule, this habit is easy to form. First, look at whether or not you are packing too much into your morning. Are you too tired and push the snooze button one time too many? Are you searching for homework and school bags as the bus rolls by? Are you scrounging for money because lunches are not packed?

Start preparing for the day the night before. Fix the kids' lunches when you are fixing dinner. Have the children complete their homework while you are fixing dinner. That way you are handy to provide help when needed. Put homework, signed papers, and money in school bags right away. Lay out clothes the night before. Have the children help you tidy up after dinner. Go to bed fifteen minutes earlier.

In the morning, each family member can rinse his or her breakfast dishes; you can wash them later. Stuck in traffic at least two times per week? Leave five minutes earlier every day. It is not really that hard to change this habit. The reward is well worth the effort.

Maintaining a Work Schedule

Working when you are scheduled should be a standard for anyone, but especially for anyone who is working as though the Lord were the employer. Workplaces should be comfortable and enjoyable, but that does not mean you can take advantage of an employer by spending too much time socializing on the job. Use your breaks and lunches for these purposes.

In today's offices, e-mail and access to the Internet are commonly available for many jobs. It is not unusual for employers to allow personal use of the Internet during breaks or after work. Most employers will allow personal calls and e-mail as long as they are minimal. A good worker does not abuse this privilege by overuse of the Internet, or tying up the phone or e-mail with personal use during work hours.

A rarely discussed issue is scheduling time off. Some people believe that if they work without ceasing they will be rewarded, and in some cases that is true. Some workaholic bosses do reward other workaholics. Other people fear that they will have too much to catch up on if they take time off, or that they may lose their jobs if they take a break. In order to keep your health and sanity you need to take scheduled time off. You have too many obligations to balance to forsake this privilege. Although a boss may be reluctant to allow the time, in most full-time positions you earn vacation time and are entitled to it. A good boss will appreciate the fact that you are taking care of yourself because it will mean fewer sick days.

Really establish your reputation at work. There is a bias out there that single moms aren't dependable. But once established, you are granted a lot more flexibility. (Cecelia; Spokane, Washington)

An accommodating job is very important to your survival. Some women cannot adapt to an 8:00 to 5:00 job because they need more flexible hours. There are many creative ways to accommodate a flexible schedule but it may mean sacrificing pay and benefits. You need to explore the obstacles and benefits to the flexible work environment in order to succeed. If this fits your priorities and you believe that God is leading you to flexible employment, it can work. It has for other mothers.

I am a hairstylist and I decided to take a cut in pay and become self-employed so that I could be in charge of my own work schedule. The Lord blessed me with my own shop and for the first six months I brought my son to work with me. (Glynda; Nacogdoches, Texas)

I basically worked or attended school while [my children] were sleeping. As they grew, I would work jobs that allowed me to work when they were in school. And I took jobs like child care for other parents in order to be able to raise my children with the values that I wanted to instill. So yes ... I have cleaned toilets, even with a master's degree, and I have taken landscaping jobs that allowed me to be flexible and work early morning hours. Was it easy? Absolutely not, but I have very fond memories of my children and can take credit for raising them. I basically trust God to take care of my career and not worry about the career ladder. (Rebecca; Walpole, New Hampshire)

I work twelve-hour shifts, mostly on weekends because I home school. My son still gets to go to church A.M. and P.M. on Sundays, midweek, and home school weekly functions. (Sherial; Dayton, Texas)

When my husband first left, God was gracious and gave me a job where my kids were, in a Christian school. When the teaching door was closing, I decided to pursue my heart's desire as an artist. I earn less than poverty, $10,000 yearly, with no child support, but I'm debt-free and happy! (Georgia; Winter Park, Florida)

Conquering the Child Care Dilemma

One of the biggest issues for working single parents is finding quality child care, especially for single moms who have jobs with unusual hours. Most mothers who would have to pay for child care either qualify for low-income government assistance, have a family member who will care for the children, care for other children in their home, swap child care, or have children who are old enough to stay home alone. The rest struggle to find good care at a reasonable price. For some families that need full-time care, this expense can consume up to half their take-home pay. Until the child-care issue is settled, it is hard to begin to concentrate on your job.

Many working mothers would rather be home parenting their children themselves. Whether married or single, working mothers struggle with the issue of finding someone they can trust to help care for their children. Carrying the entire responsibility makes it especially difficult for single moms.

My greatest challenge in adapting to work when the kids were young was having to leave them in day care and feeling that they were getting the remains of me and my day instead of the best of me. (Debbie; Delta, Colorado)

Leaving children with strangers is hard. It is not unusual for working mothers, whether married or single, to feel guilty about leaving their children. There are some questionable child-care providers. In addition, many single mothers cannot afford the kind of care that they consider safe and healthy for their children.

Know who you are leaving your children with for child care and what kind of influence is being brought into your children's lives. A godly influence is very important, especially if you cannot personally be there. (Lisa; Earlville, Illinois)

If you still need help finding child care after asking friends, neighbors, and church members, ask for a list of providers in your area from state and local agencies such as the child care licensing agency, family services, or the Better Business Bureau. Make sure that the values that are taught do not contradict the values you are teaching at home. Look for an in-home caregiver if you are not satisfied with the offerings at local centers. Be sure to check them out thoroughly! When you must leave your children, try to find the best care possible, care that reinforces your own beliefs. It may be more affordable than you think.

One of my priorities for [my son] was that he attend a Christian school where he would be taught by Christian values and receive discipline, when necessary. If at all possible, enroll [your kids] in a Christian day care or school. Some of these are really affordable; many even offer monthly tuition payments to make payments easier. Most Christian schools also offer before- and after-care at reasonable rates. (Beverly; Brentwood, Tennessee)

Getting Creative

Finding quality care isn't the only issue. When a parent works outside the home, they often miss special parent events in their children's lives that can never be recovered, such as first steps or first words, ball games, recitals, programs, or awards banquets. Most parents in two-parent families miss some of these things, but usually one parent can be involved when the other is not available.

As a single mom, you are most likely not going to be able to be there for everything your child does, but you can find ways to be more creative with child care that will allow you to save money and be more involved in your children's activities. Swapping child care with another mother who has an opposing shift will save both of you money and allow another parent to be there for your child.

Instead of paying for a baby-sitter, try to find someone you can trade baby-sitting with. (Anna; Lawrenceville, Georgia)

Staying at home with your own children is possible when you decide to make caring for children your career.

I decided to start a child care because my children had always had me with them. (Cheryl; DeSoto, Kansas)

If you are paying for the care of your children, you realize that there is no break in cost if your child is sick. You do not receive a rebate for missed days of care. You may risk losing a job if you take off work to stay home with a sick child. You may have to pay another caregiver to stay home with your child so that you can work. Either way it is costing you double for care. Even those who have children in school face a dilemma when the child needs to go home because he or she is sick.

There are various ways to prepare for this emergency. One way is to establish a relationship with a grandparent-type mentor.[2] Ideally, this would be a stay-at-home person who would spend time getting to know the child and parent and be available to pick up and keep the child in an emergency.

Due to some circumstances where schools may close early, always, always, have at least two to three people as a backup on hand. Keep their names and numbers handy in case of an emergency. Talk to them beforehand to get their permission. (Tammy; Kensington, Maryland)

Home-Based Business Solution

Caring for children is not the only option for a home-based business that allows you more time with your children. Women are operating successful businesses in many areas. Some who are gifted with sales ability are making a living at direct sales. Some are successful at providing services, such as a shopping service for busy or homebound people, a cleaning service, or aide to shut-in services. Computer skills are providing jobs in the areas of word processing, Web site design, and computer technology. Creative people are making a living at freelance writing, drafting, and promotion and advertising lay-out and design. If you have a skill, it may be marketable and could be your ticket to staying home to work.[3]

Here are a few things to consider when starting a home-based business. Most entrepreneurs start two to five businesses before they find one that works for them. In addition, it can take two or more years before a home-based business is developed enough to generate enough income to be your primary source. So keep your day job until the business is established.

Advancement Attitude

If you are already a hard worker with a great work ethic, you may merit a promotion. It is very difficult to keep your balance when that promotion is given to another. Keep in mind that promotion comes from the Lord. God is the one who gives favor and places authority. Your responsibility is to do the best job you can do. Follow all the rules. Exceed professional expectations. Try to understand and work with different personalities. If you are faithful and God's plan is for you to have a promotion, he will give you favor for the right position.

If you don't get the promotion, then it may not have been in your best interest to have it. It may have required more time, energy, and emotion than you have to give. It may have hindered time with your children, with God, or with other supportive relationships.

Don't let work/career cause you to lose your sense of priorities, and do all possible not to take the stress home. [My] church helped me set my priorities straight and showed me ways to stick to them. (Marlanges; Eden Prairie, Minnesota)

God knows what is best for you and your family. He has a plan. Seek him and keep your eyes on the lighted path. Don't give up. You will make it.

Eight

Financial Gear: Assessing Money Management Pitfalls

Pursuit of money to support the family is the most common reason single moms wear themselves out. Most of us are not prepared or equipped financially or physically to handle the demands. We didn't volunteer for the role of single parent, and we don't get much financial reward for it. We believe that we could handle it much more easily if God would just drop money in our lap. An instant win on a game show looks pretty easy, but even in game shows there's no guarantee you'll get the money.

In the reality TV show *Survivor*, contestants volunteer to be pitted against one another in a remote, rugged area with few supplies. Yet only one winner gets the million-dollar prize. Contestants are tested to be sure they are up to the challenge. I had the opportunity to hear a "survivor" from the second round of episodes speak. He said contestants were given little information to prepare for the event. They were able to take only one approved personal item and a few clothes—nothing else. These people faced tremendous obstacles, some due to the location of the contest, others due to the stress of competition.

Apparently viewers love to watch this human struggle from the comfort of their living rooms. What I find remarkable is that these contestants volunteer for the show when they have a 95 percent chance of losing.

Unlike game show contestants, many single parents are struggling with some very real obstacles for which they didn't sign up. There is no test to find out if they are prepared to handle these obstacles. Many single parents come to the job with little more than the clothes they are wearing. In addition to all of this, they come with little ones that depend on them for survival. And no one is going to reward them with a million-dollar prize.

Instead, as a single parent, you have to balance making a living, getting ahead in your job, raising kids, paying bills, fixing things that are broken, and managing a home and family activities, all while maintaining personal relationships with God and people. It is quite a feat.

You may look at the high-profile celebrity single moms and reason that if you had more money, you would have fewer struggles. High-income mothers seem to be better equipped for the journey. Even those with middle incomes often seem better equipped, because they usually have higher levels of education and already established careers when they become single moms. It may seem as though you are doomed to failure if you have to start at the bottom with limited education and little or no work experience. The amazing thing is that I have seen women at all income levels be successful.

Although none of us feel equipped when we start single parenting, low-income mothers do come to the job more ill-equipped than others. These moms are starting with an uneven playing field. Most of them are introduced to single parenting by abandonment. Because they didn't plan on their situations, they often have a tendency to blame others. If they have no other person to blame, they may blame God.

As a low-income single parent, Hazel struggled under financial pressure to the point that she "secretly resented the Lord because I could not make ends meet." This mother of six bravely decided to leave welfare when her three youngest (triplets) were three years old.

I was determined my children would not be a statistic and another welfare family. It made things harder for me but my children grew up with a real sense of self-esteem and a healthy respect for hard work. Resenting God for my struggles was a big mistake. I really didn't understand God's love for me and my family and his willingness to be everything we needed. As a result of not understanding his love, I felt even more isolated as a single parent. (Hazel; Auburn, California)

This mother did not come equipped to succeed in the traditional sense. She was a welfare mom. But she was equipped with the tools she needed to survive when she stopped blaming others and God for her situation and began to recognize what God had provided for her.

Dollars and Sense

You may think, *If I had more money, I would be able to make it.* Whether you make a lot or a little doesn't really matter. It is how you handle the resources you have that is important to your survival.

Struggling with high living expenses and debt can overwhelm you and drain all your resources. In my work I regularly see both the good and the bad results of single parents' financial decisions. One of the biggest mistakes I see is not having a spending plan. If you don't have a budget and you depend on credit as a buffer, you will be in financial trouble. For many moms it is a matter of learning to manage their resources. For others it is a matter of not having enough.

A Little Help From Friends

If your income is low, good money management may not be enough. You may need the help of others. Churches are helping people in need more today than when I was raising my children. It is encouraging to hear from parents who have received help from their churches. However, many single parents are left alone to deal with their situations because they either went to the church for help and felt rejected or misunderstood or they didn't go for help because of pride or shame.

Your own expectations may hinder your asking for help. You may expect people to reject you or judge you. You may have been rejected or judged in the past and don't want to attempt to ask again. You may expect others to do more than they should. Or you may deny any assistance that is offered because you don't want to be considered "needy."

Many single-mom families are living at or near the poverty level of income. It is a great struggle to make ends meet. Yet even if you are not living in poverty, it is easy to feel poor when you can't pay your bills, do something fun once in a while, or get something your child needs.

You don't have to be desperate or in poverty to need help. Everybody needs help from time to time. You are doing a job that is meant for two people. Right now you need help. When you come to grips with this, you will be able to get over the "needy" feeling.

Don't let the spirit of poverty or the spirit of neediness overtake you. You have the power through the Word of God and through the Lord, and need to use it. (Leah; Alpharetta, Georgia)

If you have a need, you have to overcome your pride and ask for help. Although God says that he will provide for you, he often uses people to do it.

If you need help ... don't hesitate to ask. This is especially important for the church. They cannot help when they don't know the need. I have to admit I didn't ask and they didn't offer. But we have to humble ourselves and swallow some pride and ask. We have to remember that this need gives God the opportunity to use whom he chooses and it will be rewarding for them also. (Marie; Melbourne Beach, Florida)

Take all the help you can get! Make your needs known! People cannot help if they don't know what you need. Pray. Pray. Pray. Read all you can about wise money management. (Bonnie; Toms River, New Jersey)

One way to overcome your hesitancy in asking for help is to consider how you would respond to someone else in need. Most likely, you would be more than willing and even consider it a blessing to be able to help. Currently God has given others abundance so they can help provide for your need. Down the road God may give you the resources or the opportunity to help others.

Who's in Charge?

Even at the lowest income levels, it is possible to make a financial plan work. The first step is learning what God says about managing your resources. One of the primary principles you need to understand as a Christian is that God owns everything. You are merely the steward. I found it a great relief to realize that it all belongs to God. He knows much more what to do with it than I do. I admit that it was hard to trust God's provision when I couldn't pay bills or get something the children needed. I struggled with my inability to provide and with how God provided. I wanted *him* to make *me* look good. I wanted good credit and the money to pay my bills on time. I hear from many moms for whom God has provided in that way. Yet in my case, it didn't work that way. So I often thought that I was doing something wrong or God didn't care. Neither was true. I did have some lessons to learn and suffered some consequences due to poor choices, but God was not punishing me. It was simply that his way was not my way.

Other mothers have learned the same principle. Sometimes they have seen God provide when they could not and at other times they could not see how God was providing.

I was a single mother of four children and never made over $15,000. We went for years with little or no child support. I began an in-home day care center. We ate simply, used the food bank from church, and eventually made the decision to quit food stamps. We lived debt-free. (Nora; Fort Wayne, Indiana)

The Practice of Tithing

The first step in recognizing God's ownership of all your resources is to tithe. Tithe means one-tenth. It is the measure used in the Bible to describe what God expected as a minimum offering from his people. This tithe was for the individual, not for God. God didn't need the money. He wanted their hearts. He wanted them to freely acknowledge what he had provided for them. There were three tithes mentioned in the Old Testament. The first two were to support the church and the priests. Interestingly, the third tithe, which was taken every three years, was for the widows and orphans and other needy people in the church and community. We need that tithe in the church today!

Current custom is for the tithe, which is usually considered to be 10 percent of gross income, to be given to the local church that meets the spiritual needs of the believer. Offerings are given above the tithe to needy causes as God leads. God expects Christians to be generous and give according to how much he has blessed them. The goal should be giving a minimum one-tenth of our income as a tithe according to our own hearts.

One of the biggest mistakes you can make is not recognizing God's provision through a tithe. This is the way we recognize that God owns everything and we are merely stewards of his blessings. However, most Christians tithe much less than 10 percent. Tithing is such a hard issue for so many people.

Most single parents can't imagine giving a full 10 percent of their income to God and still being able to provide for their families. They often suffer guilt because they believe that they are cheating God. Yet, statistically, lower-income families surpass middle- or higher-income families in their giving.

In America, average- or higher-income people give 2.3 percent of their incomes to charity, including to churches, each year. People who make less than $10,000 per year give almost 5 percent of their annual income to charity. Christians who sacrifice to give more do it because trusting God with their finances makes more sense than trying to figure out how to pay for everything without his help. Obviously, those who need resources the most have the greatest need to acknowledge God's ownership and provision.

No matter how hard it is, tithe faithfully. I believe God's faithfulness is the only thing keeping us afloat. (Monika; Arvada, Colorado)

Read Scripture regularly, tithe—if not a full tenth—whatever you can. God knows your heart. (Kathy; Swansea, Illinois)

God wants cheerful givers. You needn't feel guilty if you currently are giving less than 10 percent of your income to God's work. God understands the pressure on your family finances and your willingness to give more. He wants you to give out of gratitude. Your faith will grow as you witness his provision and you will gratefully give more. In fact, I think that single-parent families make the best givers because they have needed so much and want to give back and help others.

I always tithed. Even in the worst times, I never missed paying a bill nor was I ever late. Only God can do that—considering the number of times I was out of work. (Bonita; Matthews, North Carolina)

Continue to tithe. I know, I know it seems impossible—but Luke 1:37 tells us differently. I'm not 100 percent faithful to tithing my money yet, but I'm getting better. I'm like Peter when he was walking toward Jesus on the water—as long as I keep my focus on the Lord and not on my circumstances, I'm fine! But look out if I take my eyes off the Lord for just a second! I'm drowning! (Tamy; Chambersburg, Pennsylvania)

I am still low-income at $17,000 a year, but we live as though we have twice the income. When you tithe, the money multiplies. (Kristy; Pueblo, Colorado)

Lifestyle Choices

I've said it before and I'll say it again: your income really doesn't matter. God has already made provision for you. Yet nothing will defeat you faster financially than comparing yourself with others or with your old lifestyle.

Income drops 25 to 40 percent for women going through divorce. Many divorcing women bring debt from the marriage into their single-parent life. Bankruptcy among divorced women has skyrocketed. If you were married you may have enjoyed having someone help you care for the children, bring in income, pay bills, cook, clean, repair things, do yardwork, care for the car, run errands, or afford recreational activities and other luxuries. After the divorce you may be struggling to provide these benefits.

Widows whose spouses did not leave adequate provision face the same lifestyle changes. Never-married parents who have lived independently or in the comfort of a shared home with either parents or boyfriend face a considerable change in lifestyle. For most single parents, keeping up the old lifestyle is no longer financially feasible.

The most common reason for trying to keep the same lifestyle makes sense. Children suffer when one parent is no longer in the home. They lack the provision and protection of the missing parent. They will miss the benefits of the income that parent provided. They will miss having the daily care of another parent in the home. They already have to make major adjustments, so to avoid even more adjustments, many women try to maintain what they call a "normal" lifestyle, keeping the same home and keeping the children involved in the same activities.

I hated [my son] to "suffer" by seeking a small apartment or townhouse. Instead, I scraped up what little money I had (the divorce was lengthy so I didn't get any financial assistance for almost a year) and bought a fixer-upper house complete with a swimming pool and large yard. The house ended up being a money pit. It also took much of my time to maintain. I was not a handyman kind of woman and often broke down in tears trying to learn to do my own repairs. (Kathleen; Jupiter, Florida)

Many survey respondents expressed regret over keeping the same house to provide stability for their children, only later to lose the house due to finances. Even those who could afford the home couldn't afford the time and expense of keeping up the neighborhood standards. Cutting the grass, repairing roofs, cleaning gutters, trimming trees, painting houses or trim takes strength, energy, money, and time. Many women find themselves frustrated or in tears because there is one more thing they have to figure out how to fix or do. They are so burdened with activity they can't take the great pleasure of stopping to enjoy their children.

Because they don't want them to suffer further, mothers tend to try to maintain the children's preseparation activity level in sports, lessons, and church. But unless you have great support from your ex, family, or friends, this can be overwhelming for a working parent. The cost alone of activities is enough to stress a single mom, but you also have to get them to practices or games, pay for uniforms or costumes, help with snacks, and attend awards parties or recitals. If you have more than one child, it can be exhausting and expensive.

The Issue of Child Support

One of the greatest financial mistakes custodial parents make is not pursuing child support. You have a responsibility to make sure you have the resources to raise your child. Your child came into this world with two parents. Unless the father has died, he has a responsibility to support his child.

This needs to be stressed because one-third of the custodial parents eligible for child support do not have a child support order.[1] Nearly half the parents that do have support orders do not receive the full amount. The reasons for this vary, but it is important to note that even if you do have a support order, you cannot depend on it for your monthly living expenses because at some point the support may not be there. The father could lose his job, become incapacitated and unable to work temporarily or permanently, or just move to another city. In many cases it takes time to reestablish a support order.

As the custodial parent, you should do everything in your power to make sure your child has the provision of child support. The only times that you should consider not further pursuing support is when there are incidents of physical danger to you or your child or when you have earnestly sought support and it is impossible to establish or maintain due to the actions of the father. You may be entitled to the support but you may be hurting the family more by continuing the pursuit. I have seen some mothers spend more on finding the father to collect payments than they would have received in support. In situations of great threat or tremendous expense, you may have to turn to God alone as your provider and let it go.

I receive no child support and never have. I have several single mom friends who do receive support. When their exes don't pay, it kills their budgets! I have learned to live on what God provides—not my ex-husband. (Maria; Warner Robins, Georgia)

Single moms have come up with some creative strategies for keeping the support coming. One mom wrote that she took a settlement at the time of her divorce rather than monthly support payments. This strategy won't work with all situations, but it is something to consider. Most mothers establish a court-ordered payroll deduction that is taken from the father's pay.

The biggest decision I made early on was that I was not going to depend on the child support forever. I made a promise to myself that I would work hard and get to the point the child support was "extra." It was hard—very hard—and lots of hot dogs later I reached and exceeded my goal. (Dawn; Dothan, Alabama)

Try to set up child support as a percentage of the other parent's check, not to fall below a certain amount, rather than a straight amount. This way the child support goes up automatically each year as the other parent's pay goes up with each raise. This can avoid repeated court battles and expenses getting your children's support raised. (Single mom; Lawrenceville, Georgia)

Again, no matter how well your support is established, if the non-custodial parent faces a layoff, takes a new job, or moves to another city, it may put an abrupt end to regular support. You would do well not to count on this income to cover your regular monthly expenses.

I always know that God will and does take care of me and my daughter. I received child support for only two or three months and have always believed and tell others that God is my provider. I know it sounds very "spiritual," but it is my reality. (Marlanges; Eden Prairie, Minnesota)

Financial Forgiveness

Many moms hold resentment against the absent father because he seems to prosper while the single mom and the children seem to suffer. Anger is part of the grief cycle, but grief has to come to an end eventually. Attitudes of envy toward others or resentment toward the dad will hurt you and your kids much more than your lower standard of living.

Studies have shown that bitterness will cause you illness and that your attitudes, good and bad, are passed down to your children. You may have been thrust into this single-parent lifestyle and believe that it is not fair to you or your children. You're right; life with only one parent in a family is not fair. God understands that. The sooner you can take this grief to him and be healed from it, the sooner you and your children can accept what you can't change anyway. Learning to be the best mom you can be and to be content with what God has provided will take all your time and energy. You don't need to be spending it in bitterness and blame. If the other parent is still living, let God handle him.

Hanging on to the past or how things should be will cause you to perceive you or your children as suffering. As discussed earlier, your tendency will be to overcompensate for the loss.

Parents need to get over the idea that their children are suffering because they live in a single-parent home. The children will survive if they don't have the latest gadget or designer clothes. Many single-parent kids grow up healthy and happy without them. Your perspective about your children's lack is what makes the difference. Teach them what is of real value instead.

In the next chapter we'll deal with how to manage the provision you have been given.

Nine

Money Survival: Handling the Rewards of a Job Well Done

A good survivalist must have a plan. Part of that plan is managing the resources that God has entrusted to you. You can't survive if you are too stressed about funds to function. Many people fear budgeting, but a budget is simply your spending plan. A sample budget form is available in Appendix A. This form may be used to see where you are now and to make adjustments for where you need to be.

Your budget should be set up to accommodate your priorities. I can tell you that you need to give a tithe to God, but I can't make you do it. It is your responsibility to pray and determine what you believe God is guiding you to give. You will need to decide whether keeping the home is worth no vacations or after-school activities. You decide if you are willing to live more simply if you want to go to school or start a savings account to pay for emergency repairs with cash instead of credit. The old pre-single-parent plan has to go. This new plan should fit your new lifestyle.

Since this is not a book on budgeting, I am only going to provide a few guidelines on money management that will help you with your work survival.[1]

Before we begin looking at your finances, let's look at some of the reasons you may feel defeated. Because of their great need, women may pursue money or a man to rescue them, rather than looking to God and his provision. Many times they are struggling because they are in debt, they have not pursued child support, or they are trying to keep up their former lifestyle. Another big reason is fear. It is common for single mothers to fear budgeting when they know that their needs exceed their income.

The first step to budgeting is finding out where you are. That means writing it down. This was hard for me. I knew that I didn't have enough to pay everything, so I didn't see any reason to write it down. It would just depress me further. However, I eventually discovered that if I didn't begin by writing it down, I didn't know what to pray for or what I really needed.

In those very low-income years, I was afraid to look at the reality of my situation. I knew that I could manage my resources if I had more money. Yet it was easy to see that my very low income would not cover my basic expenses. So why bother? After a strong nudging from the Lord, I gave in and wrote it down. It was depressing. On paper, there was no way that we would make it. It would take a miracle. As I have shared, though, God did perform miracles for our family. I would never have known how big the miracles were if I had not taken that first step and written it down.

Benefits of a Financial Plan

Judging from comments made by some of those 150 women who responded to my survey in 2001, I am not the only one who found value in budgeting.

Set up a budget. It helps to curb some of the impulse buying and helps you see when God answers prayer for your daily needs. (Charlene; Lehigh Acres, Florida)

I began listening to [Larry Burkett's] radio program and sent away for budgeting materials. Long story short: I no longer carry a balance on my credit card, and my goal is to have my house totally paid for before I reach age sixty. I tithe on my income and I'm helping to support another single parent, as she is this year finishing her teaching degree. God has provided everything I need, most of what I want, and many of my desires. He continues to see my small family prosper financially. Bottom line: Single parents must get on a budget and tithe! (Kathleen; Jupiter, Florida)

Going through a Crown [adult small-group financial]
study changed my perspective about money.
Knowing that God owns it all gives me peace. God
has really become my husband (Isaiah 54:4). I ask him
what would be the best way to use the money he
gives us. I'm finding we have more money to give.
(Mary; Mishawaka, Indiana)

Assume you'll be single the rest of your lives and
make long-term plans, like buying a home, taking
vacations, saving for retirement. In other words,
don't put your lives on hold until Mr. Right comes
along. (Wanda; Ames, Iowa)

According to these quotes, my respondents (as recipients of a Christian financial advice newsletter) had not only heard about the benefits of budgeting, but have put the teaching into practice. Their experience[2] reiterates many of the ideas we have discussed and will be very helpful to your financial survival.

If you can't pay cash for it, save up until you can. Try
to own only one credit card, for emergencies only.
(Imogene; Norcross, Georgia)

Learn where to squeeze. Some areas of your budget just have no flex—you have to pay rent and utilities and some insurance. But you can adjust food, clothing, and recreation. (Gail; Davenport, Iowa)

Always stay a step ahead and have a plan for everything. You have to be able to map out projected expenditures and events as much as possible so you are not stressed at the last minute. (Angela; Norcross, Georgia)

Getting the Kids Involved

Encourage the children to help stretch dollars. This will train them to deal with their own finances in the future. Just be careful not to place on them the burden of meeting your adult responsibilities. Let them help according to their age and ability.

Effectively communicate the spending priorities to your children and tell them you expect their support. (Paulette; Mobile, Alabama)

> *One of the things I did do right was to have my son write all the checks for the bills and do the math so he knew what we didn't have. He also became the shopper for our needs. He would check all the ads and decide where to buy what to help save money. He had two paper routes and at age sixteen took on a job on top of that as a busboy at an Italian restaurant with the benefit of being able to take me there on my birthday for free. (Franque; El Paso, Texas)*

No matter what your income level, it is possible to make it work. The key is to place all that you have in God's hands. It belongs to him anyway and he knows much more what to do with it. Then be willing to listen to his leading. That means being willing to makes changes to fit your new lifestyle. Every area of the budget can be adjusted. Some areas may concern you more than others.

A simple budget means taking into account the various budget categories, allocating resources according to priorities, and becoming disciplined in spending according to the set guidelines. A list of budget considerations is available in Appendix B.

Here we will look at the top five areas of concern for most moms, which are usually housing, food, child care, transportation and entertainment.

Keeping the Home

What are your priorities for housing? Can you afford to keep the home you are in? Are you keeping the house for security reasons or are you trusting God for security?

Nancy is a single mom of three children. Her husband left her with a mortgage that she could not afford. The church helped her with utility bills and repairs, but it was not enough. She had an ongoing illness that kept her from working a full-time job. Hospital stays and treatments were adding to her financial pressures. Yet she wanted to keep the home because her children were teenagers and were involved with church and scouts in the area. She started a home-based business, but did not make enough to compensate for her husband's missing income.

We discussed the possibility of selling the home before foreclosure but the house was not in condition to sell. She ended up losing her home this past summer. She took two of the children to her mother's home in another county, while her oldest son stayed with his scoutmaster in their former community.

If this mom could have understood the ramifications of keeping the home, she might not have lost it in this way. Many single mothers have struggled with the issue of whether or not to keep the home.

Don't hold on to a house to keep things steady for the kids. My house was worth so little by the time I sold it, it was heartbreaking. [The money] paid my debts and legal bills with nothing left over. (Kathleen; Warrensburg, New York)

Although some people are better off selling or moving, others find creative ways to keep and afford their home. Some people are able to find better-paying jobs. Some increase an already existing home-based business or start a small home-based business to add to their income. Others have brought in boarders to share living expenses. Still others have made the sacrifice and moved in with other individuals or families. What will work for you depends upon your resources, willingness to make changes, and God's direction.

One way I was able to stretch my budget was to rent a room to a Christian person. (Fern; Fredericksburg, Virginia)

The first year after my husband left, I lived with friends. Knowing that we had to sell our home for financial reasons after my husband left, I began to explore options of living arrangements. I found a couple that I knew had been married ten years and had no children of their own. They had had other people live with them before—but never three teenagers! This was truly a gift I received from the Lord. (Becky; Lincoln, Illinois)

Some moms will compromise their values to live with someone of the opposite sex just for financial reasons. This is the easy way out. It is not trusting God. It is against God's direction for your life. It is a sure way to be out of God's will.

I was blessed to be able to afford my own place the entire time I was single. God always provided and I honestly feel that it is damaging to kids to have their parent "live with" their boyfriend. (Marie; Melbourne Beach, Florida)

God has a place for you and your children. The key is to seek him and set and keep your priorities.

Cleanliness

Whatever your housing arrangement, you will have to deal with the issue of balance. Someone said that cleanliness is next to godliness. Cleanliness is important, but if you are obsessed with a clean house, you won't have the energy for all your other demands. When I was married, my home was spotless. It was an area I could control, and I was obsessive in keeping it clean. Yet when I divorced, I couldn't keep it up. It depressed me. My counselor gave me a plaque for my wall that said, "Cleaning and dusting can wait till tomorrow, but children grow up, we've learned to our sorrow." I had to learn, as other mothers have, that spotless is not necessary.

I was too particular about my own home. I know it needs to be clean but not spotless. I should have spent more time playing and enjoying my children. (Loretta; Waynesboro, Pennsylvania)

> *If the house can't be sparkling all the time, that's OK.*
> *Don't sweat the small stuff. Make sure the kids help.*
> *There are things they can learn to do. We have a*
> *"honey do" list committee at church for people*
> *without "honeys" and this really helps. (Regina;*
> *Gainesville, Georgia)*

> *You have to learn that no one will die if your bed is*
> *not made every single morning and you forgot to*
> *pick up the milk on the way home from work. And*
> *you are not a bad mother if you are not your child's*
> *room mother or cannot attend every PTA/PTO meet-*
> *ing. (Kelly; McDonough, Georgia)*

Simplify, Simplify

One way to eliminate some of the time you have to spend on cleaning is to have fewer things! This isn't profound, I know, but it works. Getting rid of junk helped me stop obsessing. I hated finding places for things anyway.

> *De-clutter your home so you have less to clean, fix, pay*
> *for, and trip over! (Jennifer; Johnson City, New York)*

> *I think it is important to let the Lord determine what*
> *you need, instead of trying to keep up with the*
> *neighbors. I call it "don't buy the lie." You will be sur-*
> *prised how much you really don't have to have. (Gail;*
> *Davenport, Iowa)*

Take care of what you have. Use it up. Wear it out. Make do. Do without. (Ellie; Medford, Oregon)

After you get rid of the junk, simplify your life by organizing what you have left. Involve the children in this organization and the maintenance of it. If you can take a course on organizing your home, do it. Or purchase or borrow a book on the subject. One single mom who is an expert on organization shares this tip.

Organization helps your peace of mind, stress level, and teaches excellent life skills for your entire family. Try tackling one area of your home at a time, or even one item, such as a drawer in the kitchen. It's best to do the area most used first so that the benefits of organization can be enjoyed right away. We always put stuff back where we got it. This saves valuable time looking for something, and money spent on replacing something you have but can't find. (Meghan; Gainesville, Florida)

Feeding the Family

Part of maintaining a good home is feeding your family. Unless your family qualifies for food stamps, this area may be the category that gets shortchanged when funds are low. After my father died, my mom always put bills before groceries. The only time she splurged was when there was a birthday or holiday. Because we had such a low priority on nutrition, my brothers, sister, and I grew up to have weight management problems.

Health and nutrition are important to your survival and the survival of your children. Instead of cutting funding for this area, think of ways to stretch those food dollars.

Buy from warehouse clubs in quantity with a friend or two. Be sure the savings of buying in bulk justify the membership. Look for alternative ways to save, such as a food co-op where families buy in bulk and serve the co-op by taking turns in the distribution.

I participate in SHARE, a national organization that provides food for a nominal fee and two hours of volunteer time each month. I come home once a month with a laundry basket full of meats, fresh fruits, and vegetables, plus other surprises for only $14.50. There is no income requirement, just volunteer time. (Charlene; Lehigh Acres, Florida)

As mentioned earlier, some mothers find it more cost- and time-effective to do weekly or monthly cooking all at once. This can be quite an event. Be sure to include the children and some friends.

Cook more, less often. I bought groceries once a month and cooked for an entire day—meatloaf, spaghetti, taco meat, all into the freezer. I also became the crock pot queen. (Gail; Davenport, Iowa)

Child Care

We discussed this area earlier, but it won't hurt to mention it again since it's one of the biggest budget-busters for single parents. Finding safe, reasonably priced child care, especially for single moms who have jobs with unusual hours, is difficult.

In the United States, child-care costs average between $100 and $120 per week per child. If you have already researched the ideas given previously and are still going to be paying a large percentage of your income to child care, then you will need to find a way to reduce your other monthly expenses. Look seriously at your housing arrangement to see if adjustments can be made there, since that is another major contributor to a higher cost of living.

Transportation

Having a car break down is a nightmare for many single moms. Not only are they scared of being stranded somewhere unsafe, they are afraid of being without transportation. They will have to juggle dropping off and picking up the car from the repair shop, getting to and from work, transporting the children, and running errands. This usually means depending on other people because they do not have the backup at home with another car or person. Moms also tend to put car maintenance and repairs last on their list of priorities. It takes time and money to keep a car running properly. If there are more pressing needs, it is easy to push back this responsibility.

Because of these issues, single moms often overspend when

purchasing an automobile. They may believe that a newer car will keep them safer and cost less than repairing an old one. That usually is not the case. Warranty plans on newer cars do save money, but the cost of financing a car far outweighs repairing an older model. But you don't want to drive your clunker until it is unsafe.

To relieve the stress in this area of your budget, make routine maintenance a priority. If you cannot afford routine maintenance, see if your church has a car care program. If you are not a churchgoer, check local churches to see if you can locate a car care program. These Saturday car care programs usually are offered free of charge on a quarterly basis. Most programs have a lead mechanic who checks the work of volunteers and advises participants about the potential repair needs. If you need repairs, many churches have programs to help with the expenses.

Enjoyment

One of the most out-of-balance areas in a single parent's budget is the area of entertainment. A good budget should include funds for recreation. You can't live life stressed out. You have to take time to enjoy your family. So many single moms need to be told this. They are so busy surviving and their budgets are so tight that they don't take the time or spend any money on having fun. Working fun into the schedule doesn't have to mean more costly activities or expensive vacations.

If you are a single mom who is living at or near the poverty level of income, you may find it impossible to afford fun. Even if you are not living in poverty, it is easy to feel poor if you can't do something fun once in a while. There are ways to have fun without spending a lot of money.

Seek out free fun. We would take a picnic to the town park where they had free concerts once a week during the summer. Help your children learn to appreciate what they have. They do not need everything they want and they do not need it now. (Charlene; Lehigh Acres, Florida)

Parks offer a variety of opportunities for low-cost fun, from swimming and other sports to concerts. Museums usually are low-cost and were something my children and I enjoyed regularly.

Churches often offer free or low-cost activities for families. Events such as putt-putt or adventure golf are fun family outings that do not cost a lot, but they can cost even less if the church goes as a group and gets a group discount.

The most fun we had as a family was at home. We did puzzles, played school, made or cooked things, or just entertained each other with our silliness.

Most single moms do not splurge on entertainment, but on the opposite end of the spectrum are those who do spend too much on entertainment. Although they cannot afford to, they eat out way too often because of time and convenience.

Bringing this area into balance will greatly relieve the financial stress. Set a reasonable entertainment budget of about 5 percent of your net income. Use those funds to make sure you spend time with your children and have some time for yourself. This time is vital to your family's survival. Your children will remember those times with Mom much more than the things you could have bought them.

Ten
Final Thoughts

This journey you are on is temporary. It will end. Your children will grow up.

I remember thinking, *How long, O Lord?* I know some mothers balance this single-parent adventure better than others do. I personally struggled with work and finances for many years. God was always faithful, even if I was not. I have written this book as a voice of experience, not of expertise. I made mistakes and so will you. But I also learned many things along the way. I learned how to trust God in ways that I never imagined. I discovered more about who God created me to be. I learned how to be a family without a second parent in the home. I learned how to enjoy my children.

You now have the tools; how you survive is up to you. My prayer is that you will take these tools and use them not only to survive, but to thrive. These are tried and true tools you can trust. Many single moms have been where you are. They have succeeded and so can you.

Appendix A

Budget Worksheet[1]

Note: See Appendix B for budget considerations for each category. Round amounts to whole dollars.

Income per month

Salary	$_____
Child support	$_____
Alimony	$_____
Other	$_____

Total Gross Income per month $_____

Less

Tithe	- $_____
Withholding (taxes)	- $_____

Net Income per month   = $_____

Expenses

Housing	$_____
Food	$_____
Automobile/Transportation	$_____
Insurance (life, medical)	$_____
Debts (other than house or car)	$_____
Entertainment/recreation	$_____
Clothing	$_____
Savings	$_____
Medical(not covered by insurance)	$_____
Miscellaneous	$_____
School/Child care	$_____
Investments	$_____

Total of all Expenses   = $_____

Subtract Expenses from Income

Net Income per Month	$_____
Total of all Expenses	- $_____
Results (Surplus or Deficit)	= $_____

Appendix B

Budget Considerations[1]

The form in Appendix A should be used to assess where you are now and then should be adjusted after you have tracked your income for three months. If you need assistance with adjusting your budget or meeting basic expenses seek help through your local church or call Crown Financial Ministries for a referral.[2]

Here's some explanation for each category found in Appendix A. Keep in mind that this is very basic.

Income

This category includes all sources of income, including earned income, tips, gifts, child support, alimony, trusts, grants, Unemployment Compensation, Social Security, and any form of government assistance income.

Less Tithe

In your tracking budget, put the amount that you currently give to your church or to charities. When adjusting your budget, pray about the amount that you believe God would have you give.

Less Tax

On this line, enter only the amount of taxes deducted from your pay. Do not include other deductions for employer's flexible spending plan or retirement investments. There is a place to enter those amounts in the budget Expenses.

Taxes can be greatly reduced for many single moms. You may be eligible for the Earned Income Credit if your income is less than $30,000 per year and you have at least one qualifying child. This credit can net the taxpayer up to $2,500 each year whether taxes were paid or due on the federal return. Other tax considerations include use of an employer-sponsored flexible spending plan for medical expenses and child care and/or the use of the Child Care Tax Credit for those who pay for child-care expenses not included in a flexible spending plan.

There are software programs available to help you do your taxes yourself on your home computer, if you have one. Manufacturers of the software often have help tools and search engines on their Web sites. The IRS Web site has a help index and search engine, plus all of the forms available for taxpayers. You can also find IRS contact information on the site. You may still need to have a tax professional look over your return to see if you have prepared it properly. Some software programs now offer that service online. The AARP offers free tax consulting in most communities; however, their first priority is to help members and the elderly.

Net Income Per Month

This is the amount that you have to pay all of your expenses. You cannot go over this amount without going into debt. That means, to create a balanced budget, all the rest of the categories must equal no more than 100 percent of your Net Income Per Month.

Begin the budgeting process by keeping track of all spending for each budget category for a minimum of three months. This will allow you to see where you are overspending and where changes may be made.

Housing Expense Worksheet
Include all that you pay based on the monthly amount. Here's a tally form.

Mortgage or rent	$_____
Insurance (homeowners/renters)	$_____
Taxes (if not included with mortgage escrow)	$_____
Electricity	$_____
Gas/Fuel Oil (or other heat source)	$_____
Water	$_____
Trash Pickup	$_____
Telephone (in-home and cell)	$_____
Maintenance	$_____
Other	$_____
Total Housing Expense	= $_____

(A Note About Housing)
Many single moms purchase a home to provide an inheritance for children and receive a tax break. There are many programs available to help you get into housing, including programs for low-income families. However, there are some issues to consider before going into debt for a home.

Is the cost of the home and all of the above listed expenses the same or less than the expenses for renting in your area? Will you be living in the area at least five years? Are you able to save enough for a down payment and closing costs? Low-income housing assistance programs often offer alternative down payment arrangements, such as a second loan for the down payment or a very low down payment. These may help you buy the house, but will you be able to afford it after you are in it? Would you have enough equity in the home that you could sell it at a profit if there was a downturn in the economy?

Another issue is the tax break. Yes, taxes paid on a home are deductible, but only partially. You will be paying much more than you can deduct for many years. The less you owe on the mortgage, the more you will have in equity to pass on to your children.

Food
This category does not include eating out. If you pay for meals away from home at restaurants, that amount goes in the entertainment category. If you buy meals at school or work for you or your children, that goes into the school expenses category.

If you receive food stamps, enter only the amount of money you spend on food each month, not the amount of food stamps you receive or spend.

Automobile/Transportation
Other than car payments, most auto expenses are irregular expenses. Add all of the repairs, supplies, tags, insurance, and maintenance expenses that you have paid over the last year. Divide the total by twelve to get a monthly estimate. Regular

maintenance will greatly reduce the amount of repairs on a vehicle. If you cannot afford regular maintenance, look for a church-sponsored car care program that provides this service.

If you do not have an automobile, but pay for bus or train transportation to get to work, enter the average monthly amount you spend on the Automobile/Transportation line.

Insurance

This line is where you will enter any insurance deductions from your paycheck and any additional insurance premiums you may pay for health, life, or disability insurance for you or your children.

(A Note About Insurance)

You may be overspending or underspending in the area of life insurance. This type of insurance is only to provide for your family if you die. It is not to build an inheritance for the children.

Some considerations are: How much will it cost to finish raising your child or children if you died today? What expenses would no longer be required if you were not here, such as housing and personal expenses? What expenses would need to be added, such as support for the children's guardians? What debts would need to be paid off? Will the children's father be able to take on any of these responsibilities? Do you have assets, such as a home, that will aid in paying for some expenses?

One type of insurance that is often overlooked is long-term disability insurance. Most employers only pay for short-term disability. What would happen if you were to have a debilitating illness that lasted months or even years? If the sole provider were not able to work, your family would suffer great financial distress. This type of insurance is often available through your employer and can be paid through a payroll deduction.

(A Note About Wills)

While you're thinking about insurance, seriously consider preparing a will. Most single moms think that if they don't have many assets, a will is not needed. That is not true.

One of the biggest considerations you have is who will care for your children if you die. If you don't decide now, a court may decide for your children later. Is the father going to take full responsibility? If the father is not involved, are there other family members whom you would prefer to parent the kids?

A will also requires that you take a full assessment of your assets and asset distribution upon your death. Do you want the children to have that special antique from your mother or do you want it sold to cover your debts? There are will kits and booklets available in bookstores and on the Internet. However, make sure any document you prepare is reviewed carefully by a qualified attorney and probated properly in court.

Debts

This includes credit cards, debts to friends or family members, loans, second mortgages, mortgage loans, or any other debt. If you are struggling with debts, seek help through a qualified consumer debt reduction agency. This is not a lender who wants to sell you a debt consolidation loan or second mortgage. This type of agency usually charges a small fee to contact your creditors and handle repayment for you. Qualified agencies have established relationships with creditors that sometimes allow them to reduce the debt or interest on the debt and set up easier payments.

Entertainment/Recreation

This category includes eating out, cable or satellite TV, Internet service (unless used for business), occasional baby sitters, school and church activities, sports, and vacations. Cell phones for teenagers go in this category.

As you track your spending, you may not spend a lot on entertainment, but you may discover that eating out takes a lot of the family budget. Moms use eating out to socialize with other families or adults. They also may use it while on the run because it is easier to buy $1 burgers than to pack a meal. But those $1 burgers are not healthy food choices and they do add up. A little preparation will reduce this amount considerably. For example, swap meal preparation with another family. On your rushed night the other family could have dinner ready for your family, and vice versa. Another solution may be to pack your meals for dinner at the same time you pack your meals for lunch. After you have reduced your spending on eating out, you may have more money to spend on family entertainment.

Clothing

This is the amount you normally spend on clothing. Since this is an irregular expense, and some months are high, include the amount you spent all of last year and divide by twelve for a monthly amount.

A good way to stretch dollars for this area is to shop seasonal clearance sales and thrift shops.

Medical Expenses

These are out-of-pocket expenses that were not covered or reimbursed by insurance or flexible-income plans through your employer. If you do not have insurance, there are options to decrease this expense. There may be clinics in your community that charge fees on a sliding scale basis according to your income level. Dental clinics usually provide services to the public at a greatly reduced rate. The students are carefully supervised so the care should be of good quality.

Miscellaneous

This category covers everything that does not fit into another category, such as cosmetics, cleaning products, allowances, hair products and services, subscriptions, cash, and various gifts given throughout the year.

The miscellaneous category is also where legal expenses go. Establishing child support and making adjustments to the support order or child custody agreement could mean major legal expenses for a single mom. An option many moms attempt is to ask the court to charge the higher income parent with the cost of the proceedings, which is usually the dad. Legal Aid may be able to reduce the cost of some legal services for low-income moms, but others will have to pay for services. Churches may help with some legal needs, but they may avoid getting involved with problems of alimony or other situations.

You can locate a Christian attorney by writing the Christian Legal Society at 4208 Evergreen Lane, Suite 222, Annandale, VA 22003, or calling (703) 642-1070. However, using a Christian lawyer does not guarantee a sliding scale fee or gratis services.

In this category you should also include expenses involving a pet.

(A Note About Pets)

A pet is another consideration for a single-parent family. Pets can be expensive. Initial cost may be low. Someone may give you the pet or you could adopt one through the local animal shelter, but you will still need to have it vet-checked and pay for shots. Annual checkups and shots and license for dogs or cats run between $100 and $200 per year per pet. Depending upon the size of your pet and brand of food you purchase, feeding a dog or cat costs between $20 and $30 per month, or $240 to $360 per year. You will also need to consider the cost of vet care if the pet is injured or sick. There is pet insurance available today, but that is not always cost effective. Other considerations are the cost of care for the pet when your family is away on vacation or family emergencies and the extra cost of cleaning products to keep the home fresh from pet accidents.

School/Child Care

This includes all expenses you pay for schooling for you or your children and child-care expenses you pay so that you can work. Do not include expenses paid by any scholarships, grants, or government programs.

If your family qualifies for a full or partial scholarship at the child-care center or has family members who can care for your children, you may be able to greatly reduce this expense.

Investments/Retirement

This is where you enter payroll deductions for retirement plans and any private investments or retirement plans. Most single parents have little or no investments so this category may be zero during your tracking budget. If possible, this category should be a consideration if there is any surplus in your budget.

Surplus or Deficit

For most single moms, it is not unusual for the initial tracked budget to show a deficit. After evaluating your expenses, make adjustments where possible according to your priorities for your family. Again, if you cannot adjust your budget to show a surplus or at minimum a balanced budget, then seek the help of a qualified budget counselor or from the benevolence ministry at your local church.

Notes

Foreword

1. U.S. Census Bureau, press release cb98-228.html, www.census.gov, April 29, 1999.

ONE
The Challenge: Understanding the Obstacles

1. "Census Bureau Facts for Features," U.S. Census Bureau, www.census.gov, April 29, 1999.
2. "Census Bureau Facts for Features," April 29, 1999.
3. "Christians Are More Likely to Experience Divorce Than Are Non-Christians," The Barna Research Group, Ltd., December 21, 1999.
4. Susan Orr, "Real Women Stay Married," *Washington Post*, June 2000.
5. U.S. Census Bureau, Census Brief CENBR/97-1, www.census.gov, September 1997.
6. "American Agenda," *World News Tonight with Peter Jennings*, December 13, 1994.
7. "American Agenda," January 12, 1995.

8. Her book and information on her ministry, Single Parent Family Resources, may be obtained at P.O. Box 3926, Ballwin, MO 63022; 636-230-6500; e-mail: bschil4150@aol.com; www.singleparentfamilyresources.com.

TWO

The Buddy System: Why Two Are Better Than One

1. Statistically, remarriage (and the dating that precedes it) can be very risky business. Gary Richmond, in his *Successful Single Parenting* (Eugene, Ore.: Harvest House, 1990) supplies these statistics: Second marriages have a 24 percent success rate within five years. Third marriages succeed 13 percent of the time. Fourth marriages succeed only 7 percent of the time. Or, looking at it another way, "Statistics vary, but the best indicators are that 70 percent to 80 percent of second marriages end in divorce, compared to roughly 50 percent for first marriages," according to Theresa McKenna, in *The Hidden Mission Field* (Mukilteo, Wash.: Winepress, 1999).

2. This interpretation was taken from Strong's Concordance (Austin, Tex: Word Search software, version V, I-Exhalt, 1987-2000).

3. See, among other scriptural passages, Psalm 139: 13-16.

4. Elsa Houtz, *The Working Woman's Guide to Real Success* (Eugene, Ore.: Harvest House, 1990).

THREE

Where Are Your Buddies?
Finding the Support You Need

1. For information, call Crown Financial Ministries at 800-722-1976.
2. McKenna.

FOUR

Time Crunch: How to Fit It All In

1. "Women Are Talking About: Moms Dropping Out," *Ladies' Home Journal,* www.lhj.com, October 2001.

FIVE

Parenthood Attitude: It's All in Your Head

1. For a list of resources for single parents, call 1-800-A-FAMILY.
2. Single Parent Family Resources, P.O. Box 3926, Ballwin, MO 63022; 636-230-6500; e-mail: bschil4150@aol.com; www.singleparentfamilyresources.com; Single Parent Family Ministry Resource Center, P.O. Box 1687, Mercer Island, WA 98040; 425-277-8494.

SIX
Work Conditioning: Getting in Shape for the Workplace

1.   Editors of *The Life@Work Journal,* "Sixteen Respected Leaders Talk About Blending Biblical Wisdom and Business Excellence," *The Life@Work Book* (Nashville, Tenn.: Cornerstone / Word, 2000), 2.
2.   Crown Financial Ministries offers a full-assessment tool called the Career Direct Assessment, found at www.crown.org.

SEVEN
Work Survival: Putting It All Into Practice

1.   "Christian Working Woman" is a nationally syndicated radio broadcast. Host Mary Welchel has written much on the subject of Christian women in the workplace and uses her daily broadcast to bring encouragement and resources to women who work outside the home.
2.   For information on how to do this, see Larry Burkett and Brenda Armstrong, *More Than Baby-Sitting— Ministering Through Child Care* manual and video package (Gainesville, Ga.: Crown Financial Ministries, 2001). Many other options for creative child care are mentioned in this resource, which is a how-to manual for churches that want to help single parents with the child-care issue.

3.   There are resources available that describe the how-
        to's of a home-based business and provide many
        options for entrepreneurs, such as Donna Partow's
        Homemade Business (Colorado Springs, Colo.: Focus
        on the Family, 1992). Another helpful resource is the
        Small Business Administration.

EIGHT

Financial Gear: Assessing Money Management Pitfalls

1.   U.S. Census Bureau, *Current Population Reports*,
        www.census.gov, (P23-189), June 2000.

NINE

Money Survival: Handling the Rewards of a Job Well Done

1.   If you need help establishing your budget, call
        Crown Financial Ministries at 800-722-1976 for infor-
        mation about materials for single parents or about
        talking to one of the hundreds of lay-budget coun-
        selors across the United States.

2.   Here's another voice: "I try to make a yearly budget
        each December based upon the expenses from the
        previous year and any new expenses I anticipate for
        the following year. Whenever you receive 'extra'
        money such as tax refunds, gifts, or child support,
        spend this money wisely, and if at all possible, try to
        save this money. Shop in thrift stores. This is very

difficult for some people to do, including, at one time, myself. I finally took the plunge when I had a new baby and no money to buy her clothes. When I visited the thrift store for the first time, I was shocked. I purchased nearly thirty outfits for my daughter for under $30. The clothes were like new (in fact, some were new). They were also designer names. I later started buying for myself." (Linda; Decatur, Georgia)

APPENDIX A

1. Adapted from Larry Burkett and Brenda Armstrong, *Making Ends Meet, Budgeting Made Easy* (Gainesville, Ga.: Crown Financial Ministries, 1997).

APPENDIX B

1. Adapted from Burkett and Armstrong, *Making Ends Meet, Budgeting Made Easy.*
2. Many local churches provide benevolence programs and/or Crown programs such as small groups or classes on the principles of good money management and free budget counseling. For information on a church near you, call Crown at 800-722-1976.

Bibliography

Burkett, Larry. *The Financial Guide for the Single Parent.* Updated by Brenda Armstrong. Chicago: Moody, 1997.

Burkett, Larry and Brenda Armstrong. *Single Parent Ministry Training Manual.* Gainesville, Ga.: Crown Financial Ministries, 1997; 2000.

Burkett, Larry and Lee Ellis. *Finding the Career That Fits You.* Chicago: Moody, 1994.

Cloud, Dr. Henry and Dr. John Townsend. *Boundaries.* Grand Rapids, Mich.: Zondervan, 1992.

Editors of The Life@Work Journal. *The Life@Work Book.* Nashville, Tenn.: Word, 2000.

Houtz, Elsa. The *Working Woman's Guide to Real Success.* Eugene, Ore.: Harvest House, 1990.

Hunter, Lynda. *Parenting On Your Own.* Grand Rapids, Mich.: Zondervan, 1997.

Mackenzie, Alec. *The Time Trap*. New York: AMACOM, American Management Association, 1997.

McKenna, Theresa. *The Hidden Mission Field*. Mukilteo, Wash.: Winepress, 1999.

Rabey, Lois Mowday. *The Snare*. Colorado Springs, Colo.: NavPress, 1998.

Richmond, Gary. *Successful Single Parenting, Going It Alone*. Eugene, Ore.: Harvest House, 1990.

Schiller, Barbara. *Just Me and the Kids*. Ballwin, Mo.: Single Parent Family Resources.

Scheele, Adele. *Career Strategies for the Working Woman*. New York: Fireside, 1994.

Stoltz, Paul G. *Adversity Quotient, Turning Obstacles Into Opportunities*. New York, Toronto: John Wiley & Sons, 1997.

Welchel, Mary. *How to Thrive From 9 to 5*. Ann Arbor, Mich.: Servant, 1999.

Resources from
CROWN FINANCIAL MINISTRIES

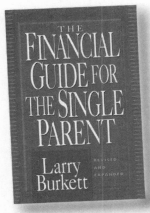

This book and workbook offer trustworthy and helpful advice on budgeting, facing the job market, understanding alimony, child support, and dealing with wills, trusts, and insurance.

The *Financial Guide for the Single Parent* is also an ideal tool for churches, ministries, and counselors who work with single parents.

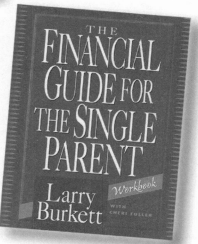

For more details and to order, visit us online at
www.crown.org
or call 1-800-722-1976